THE MYTH OF THE JEWISH MENACE IN WORLD AFFAIRS

or

THE TRUTH ABOUT THE FORGED
PROTOCOLS OF
THE ELDERS OF ZION
By
LUCIEN WOLF

Includes:

THE PROTOCOLS OF THE LEARNED ELDERS OF ZION

"*It would not be easy to say how large a part of our troubles in the present troublous times is due to the general discredit that has overtaken the old British virtue of honesty.*"

The *Morning Post*
(in a lucid interval of subjectivity),

August 28, 1920.

PREFATORY NOTE

The substance of the following three essays was originally contributed, in the form of independent articles to the *Manchester Guardian*, the *Spectator*, and the *Daily Telegraph* respectively. They have been carefully revised, much amplified, and largely rewritten in order to make a connected argument and avoid repetition. Footnotes of authorities have been added. My grateful acknowledgments are due to the Editors of the *Manchester Guardian*, the *Spectator*, and the *Daily Telegraph* for their kindness in permitting this republication.

I confess to a feeling of shame at having to write this pamphlet at all. That reputable newspapers in this country should be seeking to transplant here the seeds of Prussian anti-Semitism, and that they should employ for this purpose devices so questionable and a literature so melodramatically silly, cannot but cause a sense of humiliation to any self-respecting Englishman. It is for this reason that I have strictly limited myself to an examination of the specific charges formulated by these publications. I cannot bring myself to believe that it is necessary to deal with them on a larger scale.

L.W.

Gray's Inn, London, W.C.

November, 1920.

THE MYTH OF THE JEWISH MENACE

I
THE DEMONOLOGY OF THE "MORNING POST"

The prodigious essay on "The Cause of World Unrest" which the *Morning Post* has lately published in seventeen articles and some sixty columns of printed matter[1] is a document on which the student of political thought in England will dwell sadly. Over a century ago, in world circumstances of startling similarity and almost from the same party standpoint, Burke gave us, in his "Causes of the Present Discontents," his "Reflections," and his "Regicide Peace" a large and stately piece of political philosophy. To-day the leading organ of Conservative opinion in this country can only expound a sort of political demonology, borrowed partly from the obscurantists of Bourbon Clericalism and partly from the fanatics of Hohenzollern Anti-Semitism. It would be merciful to pass by this strange effort in silence, but unfortunately there is reason to believe that, with all its grotesqueness, it is calculated to work a good deal of mischief. Credulous and vicious people are still abundant, and they are not confined to the crowd. Mr. Winston Churchill has darkly hinted that he reads the signs of the times much in the same way as the *Morning Post*, and a curious story is current that the translation of the Russian forgery on which the theory of that journal mainly rests was actually made in the Intelligence Department of the War Office. Then there are Mr. Chesterton and Mr. Belloc and quite a conventicle of smaller fry who have been vainly preaching the same apocalypse for years. The *Morning Post* may bring them recruits, and that assuredly is not desirable.

---

[1] *Morning Post*, July 12-30, 1920.

The theory of the *Morning Post* may be briefly stated. Its fundamental contention is that all political unrest is artificial. It is a product of the Hidden Hand which is now revealed to us as a "Formidable Sect" encompassing the world. This sect has been at its present work for at least a hundred and fifty years. The French Revolution was contrived by it, as well as all the subordinate revolutions down to our own time. Trade Unionism, Socialism, Syndicalism, Bolshevism, Sinn Fein, Indian Nationalism, and their analogues in every part of the globe are outward and visible signs of its sinister activity. That there are social grievances and even evils at the root of this unrest is not denied, but they are as artificial as the unrest itself. They have all been deliberately brought about by the Hidden Hand in order to stir up revolt against the Throne and Altar. The way in which it has been done is a little complicated. Behind the restless and seditious movements which we all know there is a secret revolutionary organisation in the shape of Freemasonry. But this is only intermediate, for Freemasonry itself, through some obscure transaction between the Templars and the Old Man of the Mountain, was created by the "Formidable Sect," and is wholly, though perhaps unconsciously, under its control. Freemasonry had a specially "activist" wing in the Illuminati—also an invention of the Formidablists—which was chiefly responsible for the French Revolution.

Now, what is this "Formidable Sect"? It is no other than the Jews. Those ancient enemies of the human race appear to have been even more daring and dynamic in evil-doing than even Torquemada supposed. Throughout their world-wide Dispersion they have secretly preserved their old political organisation, and they have used it—and are still using it—with deadly persistency to overturn the established Christian order of things and to found in its place a universal Jewish dominion under the sceptre of a Sovereign of the House of David. The Jews are, in short, the "cause of the world unrest."

There is nothing new in this theory except the claim of its authors to have produced documentary proof of its final development—that is, of its Jewish aspect. *Quâ* international conspiracy, it was invented over a century ago, as it has been resurrected to-day, to explain the unfamiliar international character of the prevailing unrest. The clergy and the nobility of the *ancien régime* were as little capable as the *Morning Post* to-day of understanding the natural causes of this phenomenon. And yet they were by no means obscure. The French Revolution, as Burke pointed out, was not a mere uprising against local oppression, but a "revolution of doctrine and theoretic dogma"[2] which was bound to find echoes beyond the French frontiers. In this respect it resembled the Reformation, and also that other "armed doctrine" which we know as Bolshevism. Nevertheless it puzzled the Bourbon apologists, and, confusing cause and effect, they became convinced that they were in the presence of an international conspiracy.

The theory was first propounded by a Superior of the Seminary of Eudists at Caen in 1790,[3] but it was afterwards vastly developed by the Abbé Barruel in his "Mémoires sur le Jacobinisme," by Robison of Edinburgh in his "Proofs of a Conspiracy," and by the Chevalier de Malet in his tedious "Recherches Historiques." Their conclusion was that there was a triple conspiracy of Philosophers, Freemasons, and Illuminati, who formed an actual sect aiming deliberately and methodically at the overthrow of the established religions and governments throughout Europe. It is noteworthy that their researches failed to discern any Jewish element in this conspiracy, though in minuteness of investigation and in the gluttony of their credulity they were by no means inferior to the *Morning Post*, while they had the advantage over that journal of being in close touch with the facts. The theory had a short shrift, though the industry of its authors certainly did much to throw light on the organisation and activities of the secret societies. So far as the Freemasons and Illuminati were concerned, it was easily demolished by the Earl of Moira, who at a meeting of the Grand Lodge of England in 1800

---

[2] "Thoughts on French Affairs" (Burke's Works, Vol. III., p. 350).
[3] *Gentleman's Magazine*, June, 1794.

showed convincingly that it was a mare's nest.[4] As for the Philosophers, no one ever took the charge against them seriously. For half a century scarcely anything more was heard of this aspect of the "Formidable Sect," though meanwhile the Revolutions of 1830 and 1848 took place. The non-suit of Barruel was *chose jugée.*

It was revived in the sixties under the influence of the religious passions kindled by the war for Italian unity. The struggle for Jewish emancipation had triumphed all over Western Europe, largely as a consequence of the Revolutions of 1848, and the new citizens thus enfranchised had everywhere cast in their lot with the Liberal parties. This was swiftly and angrily noted by the Ultramontane polemists, and the old bogey of a "Formidable Sect" began to haunt them in a revised and enlarged form. In the new conspiracy there was no longer any talk of Philosophers and Illuminati. Their place was taken by Jews and Protestants. The "Formidable Sect" thus became a triple alliance of Freemasons, Jews, and Protestants, which was said to be directed by the "Grand Master Palmerston," and supported by the whole British people, not only as Protestants, but as descendants of the Lost Tribes of Israel. The chief protagonist of this stupendous hallucination was M. Gougenot des Mousseaux, who in 1869 embodied it in a volume entitled "Le Juif, le Judaïsme, et la Judaïsation des Peuples Chrétiens." From his own admissions, however, it appears that he was largely indebted to German Catholic inspiration. Once again the theory failed to find support, and Gougenot's book, like the books of Barruel and Robison, became relegated to the literature of forgotten crazes.

Later on attempts to revive it were made by M. de Saint-André, the Abbé Chabauty, M. Drumont, M. Martin, and M. Copin-Albancelli, in the full flood of the Anti-Semitic agitation which had been imported into France from Germany. The only notable addition made to the theory by these writers was the hypothesis of a secret Jewish Government, transported from

---

[4] *Infra* p. 14.

9

Jerusalem into the Diaspora, which, throughout the ages, has never ceased to command the allegiance of an imaginary international Jewry, to keep it disloyal to all other Governments, and to direct it in an insidious campaign against the established order of Christian Society. Since 1909 the agitation has become retransferred to the headquarters of Clerical Anti-Semitism in Vienna and Munich, and the most recent works on the subject—with which the *Morning Post* appears to have mainly worked, although for obvious reasons it does not acknowledge them—are Wichtl's "Weltfreimaurerei, Weltrevolution, Weltrepublik," Meister's "Judas Schuldbuch," and Rosenberg's "Die Spur des Juden im Wandel der Zeiten," all published in 1919. All this literature, while expounding exactly the same theory of a Judeo-Masonic conspiracy as the *Morning Post*, is as violently anti-English as it is anti-Masonic and anti-Jewish. A great deal of it is published under the auspices of the *Deutschland's Erneuerung* Committee, of which Mr. Houston Chamberlain is a leading spirit.

This, then, is the very dubious raw material of the theory hashed up by the *Morning Post* as a serious contribution to the grave political preoccupations of British statesmanship at this moment. It will be noted that in the forms so far reviewed it is confessedly a theory, resting at the best on evidence of a highly conjectural and circumstantial character. The novelty in its latest presentation is that an effort is made to bolster it up with what is claimed to be direct evidence. This takes the form of a document entitled "The Protocols of the Learned Elders of Zion," which was opportunely published in an anonymous pamphlet a few months ago by Messrs. Eyre and Spottiswoode. These protocols are alleged to be the minutes of certain meetings of the Secret Directory of the Jewish people held in Paris towards the end of the last century, and they pretend to record avowals by the "Elders" of the very conspiracy set forth hypothetically by MM. Gougenot des Mousseaux and Copin-Albancelli. The joy of the *Morning Post* at the discovery of this evidence is not difficult to understand. Its theory threatened to collapse under the weight of its inherent grotesqueness, and here, in the nick of time, was documentary proof, complete and apparently irrefutable. "In this book," says the *Post* triumphantly, "for the first time we find an open declaration of the terrible conspiracy of the 'Formicable Sect.'"[5]

Unhappily for the *Morning Post*, this document is a forgery, and one which has already been used for even more disreputable purposes than the bolstering up of the malicious hypothesis in support of which it is cited. The story of this forgery will be told presently.[6] For the moment I content myself with noting that it is a forgery, and proceed to examine briefly the main historical propositions which it is invoked to corroborate and co-ordinate. This is necessary not because they are in themselves worth taking seriously, but because they are held to react on the forged protocols and to supply presumptive evidence of their genuineness.

I take the propositions in the logical order of the argument they are put forward to illustrate:—

---

[5] *Morning Post*, July 16, 1920.
[6] *Infra* pp. 19 *et seq.*

I. THE SECRET JEWISH GOVERNMENT

This proposition, borrowed, for the most part, from the wild conjectures of Copin-Albancelli, has a queer flavour of the anti-Catholic bogey which was at one time so fiercely exploited by Hot-gospellers, and in which even Mr. Gladstone believed as late as 1874—the Pope standing for the Prince of the Captivity and the Syllabus for the Protocols of Nilus. What, however, is very remarkable is that the protagonists of this fantastic calumny are, for the most part, Roman Catholics who have themselves suffered from it in a form much more difficult to grapple with. The short answer to it in the case of the Jews is that it is an invention, and that not only is there no trace of it in the history of the Dispersion, but that, on the contrary, the Jews, even as a Church, and still more in their secular relations, have suffered more from the want of international organisation and uniformity than any other Church or religious community. The Princes of the Captivity, for example, were confined to the Babylonian Exile, and were little more than the local Presbyters *omnium Judæorum Angliæ* of Angevin England or the Presidents of the Jewish Consistory of modern France. The allegation that the final aim of this Secret Government is the establishment of a universal Jewish dominion under a Prince of the House of David is a curious muddle of eschatology and politics. With much better reason the early Anabaptists said virtually the same thing of the Roman Catholic Church, and, indeed, on the *Morning Post* plan of campaign, it might be retorted on all the great Churches. With the Jews it has no more to do with practical politics than the analogous hopes of pious Christendom. The *Morning Post*, however, does not stand alone in its error. A curious variant of it is found in recent German Antisemitica. The World Unrest is there pictured as due to a conspiracy of Jewry and the British Empire, based on the Anglo-Israelitish theory that the British people are the Lost Tribes and the Royal House of Windsor the authentic seed of David. Accordingly, Britons and Jews together are accused of having plotted the late war in order to fulfil the

12

Messianic prophecies in the person of King George.[7] *Les grands esprits se rencontrent!*

---

[7] See Wichtl and Meister *op. cit.* A peculiarly crazy statement of this theory, illustrated by an obscene chart pedigree of Queen Victoria, will be found in *Semi-Imperator* (Munich, 1919). *Cf.* Proceedings of the British Israel World Federation Congress, July 5-10, 1920.

2. THE OCCULT POWER BEHIND FREEMASONRY

It follows that if there is no "Secret Government of the Jewish Nation," such a Government cannot well be "the occult power which works behind Freemasonry."[8] The *Morning Post*, however, is very careful to hedge on this, as on many other points. Its alternative theory is that Freemasonry is Judaical because it is descended from the Templars, who received their Jewish traditions from the Assassins.[9] The only foundation for the suggestion that the Assassins could act as intermediaries between the Jews and the Templars is, on the one hand, that they were Ishmaelites, and consequently "first cousins" to the Jews, and, on the other, a much disputed hypothesis of Von Hammer, that certain Templars were initiated into the mysteries of the Assassins.[10] The truth is that the Assassins were not Ishmaelites, except in the figurative sense that all Mohammedans claim to be descended from Ishmael, and even if they were, they had no contact with Jews, and their tenets bear no trace of Jewish influence. Consequently, whatever else the Templars may have learnt from them, they certainly did not learn Judaism. The nearest approach to a tradition of Hebrew influence on Templarism is found in a very dubious legend of Swedish Masonry which alleges that certain Templars of Jerusalem received the secrets of the Essenes from seven Syrian Christians whom they rescued from the Saracens.[11] But if this story were true, the secrets thus taught would assuredly have been more Christian than Jewish. To anyone, however, who knows anything of mediæval history, and the relations of Moslems and Jews at this period, the whole of this conjecture is the crudest buffoonery. No section of the Crusaders dealt with the Jews except by way of massacre. Moreover, had there been the slightest

---

[8] *Morning Post*, July 14, 1920.
[9] *Ibid.*
[10] Quoted by Frost, "Secret Societies of the European Revolution," Vol. I., p. 6.
[11] Frost, *op. cit.*, pp. 12-13.

ground for believing that the Templars had Judaised it would have been seized upon as the most damning of all crimes alleged against them when the Order was suppressed. But throughout the comprehensive indictment, which ranges from the Gnostic heresy to gross licentiousness, there is no hint of the deadly sin of Judaism.

3. THE JUDAISATION OF FREEMASONRY

This, however, is not the end of the matter. Yet other historical testimonies are alleged—the Temple cultus in Freemasonry, the "Jewish Ritual" of the Order, and the direct activities of Jews in its anti-monarchical and anti-Christian machinations.

(a) The first of these arguments may best be judged by the *Morning Post's* own witnesses. Whether Freemasonry was or was not derived from the Templars and whether or not the Templars became infected with Jewish ideas transmitted through the Assassins, nothing is more certain than that the founders of Templarism established their Order on the Temple cultus long before they could have known anything of the Assassins, and while they were still impeccable Knights of the Cross. Hence, if the Freemasons took the Temple from them, it was innocent of Jewishness. But Robison—one of the main authorities of the *Morning Post*—will not even have it that the Freemasons were indebted to the Templars, much less to the Jews. He states that the theory, and even the Temple cultus, were unknown to Freemasonry before 1743, when they were introduced to them for the first time by the Jacobite, Andrew Ramsay.[12]

(b) The so-called "Jewish Ritual" of Masonry is equally a delusion, as the *Morning Post* could have found out for itself, had it taken the trouble to consult somebody who knows Hebrew and Hebrew literature. The grammatical forms and the transliteration of the limited number of Hebrew words found in the Masonic rituals prove conclusively their non-Jewish origin. The legendary matter, too, has but few traces of Jewish *provenance*, and is clearly not due to Jewish redaction. If the rituals were Jewish, one might expect to find parallel passages in the Hebrew Prayer-Book and similar literature, but nothing of the kind is discoverable. It is really remarkable that Jews had nothing to do—and indeed, I believe, never have had anything to do—

---

[12] Robison: "Proofs of a Conspiracy Against all the Religions and Governments of Europe" (Lond., 1797), pp. 38-39.

16

with the composition of the Masonic rituals, seeing that the lodges, in this country, at least, have always been open to them, and at an early date learned Jews were interested in them and possibly joined them; but so it is. The true explanation of the Hebrew elements in Freemasonry, as in Templarism, is that both borrowed from the Old Testament, as a Christian document.

(c) As for the activities of Jews in the anti-monarchical and anti-Christian machinations of Masonry, the answer is that orthodox Masonry has never been anti-monarchical or anti-Christian, and if there have been spurious lodges open to this reproach, and if orthodox lodges have been improperly used for this purpose, they were, at any rate, free of the added reproach of Jewish control or inspiration. The only evidence on this head cited by the *Morning Post*—or, rather, by Mrs. Webster on its behalf—is that a Jew known by the nickname of Piccolo Tigre issued a scandalously anti-social manifesto to the Piedmontese Alta Vendita in 1822, and that he was abetted by "others of his race."[13] We are not told who these "others" were, nor even what Piccolo Tigre's real name was. If Mrs. Webster does not know his name, how can she know that he was a Jew? The answer is that she got the story from Gougenot des Mousseaux, but even he naïvely admits that he never knew who Piccolo Tigre was.[14] And yet he is positive he was a Jew. This is typical of all the *Morning Post's* evidence.

---

[13] *Morning Post*, July 15, 1920. See also *Spectator*, June 19 and 26, 1920.
[14] Gougenot des Mousseaux, *op. cit.*, p. 343.

4. FREEMASONRY AND REVOLUTION

If the Freemasons think it worth while, they will, no doubt, reply to the *Morning Post* through a better-qualified member of the Craft than myself,[15] but, unlike the Jews, they can afford to treat the superstitions with which they are assailed with contempt. It will suffice here to quote what Lord Moira said on the subject in 1800:—

"Certain modern publications have been holding forth to the world the society of Masons as a league against constitutional authorities—an imputation the more secure because the known constitutions of our fellowship make it certain that no answer can be published. It is not to be disputed that in countries where impolitic prohibitions restrict the communication of sentiment, the activity of the human mind may, among other means of baffling the control, have resorted to the artifice of borrowing the denomination of Freemasons, to cover meetings for seditious purposes, just as any other description might be assumed for the same object. But, in the first place, it is the invaluable distinction of this free country that such a just intercourse of opinions exists without restraint as cannot leave to any number of men the desire of forming or frequenting those disguised societies where dangerous dispositions may be imbibed. And, secondly, the profligate doctrines which may have been nurtured in any such self-established assemblies could never have been tolerated for a moment in any lodge meeting under regular authority. We aver, therefore, that not only such laxity of opinion has no sort of connection with the tenets of Masonry, but is diametrically opposite to the injunction which we regard as the foundation-stone of the lodge, namely, Fear God and honour the King."[16]

---

[15] Since this was written a learned and comprehensive reply has been published, demolishing the whole Masonic side of the *Morning Post's* argument. (See A.W. Waite: "Occult Freemasonry and the Jewish Peril" in the *Occult Review,* Sept., 1920.)

[16] Oliver: "History of Masonic Persecution," pp. 298-300.

To this it should be added that Masonic lodges—more or less spurious—have not only been used by Atheists and Revolutionists for their own sinister purposes, but also by their enemies. We learn from Robison that even the Roman Catholic Church at one time tried to capture them—possibly for ends not over-friendly to the Established Church in this country—and that the Jacobites, who can scarcely be called enemies of the Throne and Altar, were extremely active in the Masonic Order during the eighteenth century.[17]

---

[17] Robison, *op. cit.*, pp. 30, 38-39, 62.

5. THE JEWISH AUTHORSHIP OF THE FRENCH REVOLUTION.

This is a pet theory of Mrs. Webster, and is very largely based on the untenable propositions noticed above. It is, however, also sought to show that the Illuminati and the Martinezists were active artisans of the Revolution, and that they were abetted by Jews. On this the only concrete evidence adduced is that Martinez Pasqualis, who figured prominently in both movements, was "generally reputed to be a Portuguese Jew." As a matter of fact, there were scarcely any Portuguese Jews at the time, and even the distinction between Old and New Christians in Portugal had been recognised as obsolete and abolished by decree in 1768.[18] Pasqualis was probably as little—or as much—a Jew as Pombal or Dom Joseph in the popular anecdote.[19] As for his alleged Jewish abettors, it is noteworthy that neither Barruel nor Robison—both contemporaries of the Revolution—knew anything of them. Barruel, indeed, ignored the theory when it was actually suggested to him, and for good reason. No one knew better than he how ludicrous it was. The Jews in Paris at the time were few and relatively insignificant; they did their duty by the new Government, but were sturdily on the side of moderation, and so far from having had any hand in making the Revolution they were actually the last to benefit by it. They were, in fact, the only class of the population whose disabilities were continued by the new régime, and it was not until September, 1791, that, after many appeals from them and in face of a strong opposition, the National Assembly consented to their emancipation.[20] As for their political opinions, they are sufficiently illustrated by the fact that one of the first acts of the Terror was to arrest forty-six of them as suspect of "délits contre-révolutionnaires"—the charge is

---

[18] Smith: "Memoirs of Pombal," Vol. II., p. 248.
[19] *Ibid.*, pp. 249-250. As a matter of fact Pasqualis was a Christian born at Grenoble (Waite: *Occult Rev.*, Sept., 1920).
[20] Kahn: *Les Juifs à Paris*, pp. 64-71.

itself a vindication—and nine of them were executed.[21] None of these good people were of any political prominence. Indeed, whether for good or evil, not a single Jewish name figures conspicuously in the history of the Revolution. With the subsequent Revolutions of 1830 and 1848 the case was different, but these were essentially bourgeois movements, and the Jewish activity in them was characteristically middle-class and moderate.

---

[21] *Ibid.*, pp. 72-85.

6. MARX, THE JEWISH REVOLUTIONARY ARCHETYPE.

The general suggestion of the *Morning Post* that the Jewish Community is, for the most part, composed of dangerous Revolutionists is a little difficult to deal with, because, at the same time, it is admitted that they are not sincere. While preaching their subversive doctrines they are said to be really anti-democratic, and to simulate a zeal for Atheism and Anarchy only in order to bring about the social and political Armageddon out of which their own Davidic Autocracy is to emerge and triumph. Everything, then, hinges on this motive, and it has already been shown that it is nothing more than a millennial hope which has no place in the field of practical politics. The appeal to Karl Marx as the Archetype of the Jewish Revolutionist is, in this connection, particularly unfortunate. In the first place, Marx was not even remotely a Jew by religion, and therefore the Messianic motive is scarcely likely to have weighed with him. He was probably a sincere Revolutionist, and, in that case, he was just as little a Jew, seeing that his philosophy has no relation to any recognised school of Jewish thought. Marx, indeed, was an intellectual product of the essentially Gentile teachings of Hegel and Feuerbach. Perhaps the best test of the Gentilism of his outlook is that, while his Jewish disciples were comparatively few, his Christian converts are numbered in millions. In the second place, if Marx was the chief instrument of a Jewish plot to subvert Christian society, he must have proved something of a disappointment to his secret employers. Among the forces which are making for World Unrest to-day he is a relatively conservative element. The *Morning Post* itself supplies the proof of this. In its anxiety to convict Marx of adding the sin of Germanism to the criminality of anti-Christian Thuggee—a little difficult to reconcile—it recalls his life-long quarrel with Bakounine, and explains it as exclusively a struggle between Judeo-Germanism and Slavism.[22] There is, however, no reason to believe that it was at

---

[22] *Morning Post*, July 16, 1920.

bottom anything but a conflict between Socialism and Anarchism—that is, between those who, however revolutionary they may be in a social sense, would still maintain the structure of the State, and those who would destroy it root and branch. Here we see that it is not the Jew Socialist who works to destroy the established political order of things, but the Gentile Anarchist. This point may be still further illustrated by Syndicalism and Bolshevism, which are both far more destructive than Socialism and are both revolts against Marx. It is true that Lenin pretends to be a strict Marxist, but his orthodoxy is vehemently contested by all the leading Marxists in England, France, and Germany, and by the whole body of Russian Mensheviks, among whom are many Jews.[23]

It is impossible, within the restricted scope of this essay, to deal with all the incidental accusations against Jews contained in the *Morning Post* indictment; but most of them will be found covered by the above classification. The charge of Bolshevism, which is the only conspicuous exception, will be examined in a later chapter.

The upshot of the matter is that the "Formidable Sect" is a German Anti-Semitic and Anglophobe myth, founded in malice and hysteria, built up of garbled history, and synthetised by impudent forgery. How it came to impose itself on the plethoric patriotism of the *Morning Post* is a mystery which may be worth investigating. Whatever the explanation, it must be counted a triumph for German junkerdom and a consoling token to that eminent traitor Herr Houston Chamberlain that he is not altogether without spiritual affinities in the land of his birth.

---

[23] *Infra* pp. 45-46.

II
THE FORGED PROTOCOLS

Chief among the *pièces justificatives* relied upon by the demonologists of the *Morning Post* is an anonymous pamphlet which calls itself "The Jewish Peril."[24] As has been stated in the previous chapter, this pamphlet is a forgery, or, rather, a garbled translation of a clumsy Russian forgery by a certain Sergyei Nilus, intended to pander to the superstition of the "Hidden Hand." There is reason to believe that it has itself been engineered by a more substantial hand reaching out stealthily from the arcanum of German Militarist Reaction.

The literary and political history of this pamphlet is quite easy to trace, though it has been a little obscured by its author's infirmities of memory. Fundamentally it belongs to a type of forgery which was common enough in the 17th and 18th centuries, when party passions ran high and the reckless scurrilities of political warfare could not be made effective without the concoction of bogus documents.[25] In our own time this fraudulent traffic has become relatively rare, though the notorious Pigott and Dreyfus forgeries are there to show how easily it may be tempted into life when malicious controversialists venture on accusations which they cannot otherwise substantiate. This is precisely the case of "Professor Sergyei Nilus," the alleged author of the Russian original of "The Jewish Peril."

His documented "discovery" that the Jews, in conspiracy with certain secret brotherhoods, are at the bottom of all the political and religious convulsions and all the social instabilities throughout the world, has been devised to bolster up a theory which has long failed to convince. The theory itself, of which the *Morning Post's* "Formidable Sect" is the latest product, is at least

---

[24] Lond., Eyre and Spottiswoode, Ltd., 1920. *Morning Post*, July 16 and 17, 1920.

[25] See Isaac D'Israeli, "Curiosities of Literature," Vol. III., pp. 143-150.

three centuries old. It was the staple of the pseudo-Apocalyptic literature of Antichrist and the Wandering Jew which assailed the early years of the Reformation and filled the literary armoury of the League during the Thirty Years' War. It took more definite political shape in the tracts and broadsheets, afterwards collected by the German Evangelical Clericals under the title of *Anabaptisticum et Enthusiasticum Pantheon,* which, among other fearsome things, explained the Puritan Revolution in England— the Bolshevism of its day—as a plot against Christianity and Monarchy contrived by the *Quäcker, Frey-Geister und Heil- und Gottlosen Juden.*[26] In the early eighteenth century its specifically anti-Jewish aspects were emphasised by the misapplied learning of Eisenmenger, whose anti-Semitic classic, "Entdecktes Judenthum," was published at the cost of King Frederick of Prussia.[27] After the French Revolution and the upheavals of 1830 and 1848, a fresh impulse was given to the agitation. Meanwhile, the Illuminati had come into existence, and Freemasonry had become known, and they were promptly annexed by the scaremongers and substituted for the Quakers and Freethinkers in their new redaction of the "Hidden Hand." A number of blood-curdling works dealing in minute detail with their supposed activities as authors of the Revolutions were published by such writers as Father Barruel (1797, etc.), the Chevalier de Malet (1817), Eckert (1854), Gougenot des Mousseaux (1860), Crétineau-Joly (1863), Saint-André (1880), and Chabauty (1883). These books all fell flat. The blood of the public refused to be curdled, and to-day they are only found in second-hand bookshops or in the libraries of collectors of Masonic and Occult ana.

In 1868 an ingenious German named Hermann Goedsche conceived the idea of galvanising the agitation into effective life

---

[26] *Anabaptisticum,* etc. (1702). See particularly the tract entitled *Erschröckliche Bruderschafft der Alten und Neuen.*
[27] Preface to Schieferl's edition (Dresden, 1893).

by giving a dramatic form to all its theoretical extravagances.[28] Formerly in the Prussian postal service, where he also acted as a spy for the Secret Police and the *Kreuz Zeitung* party, he had been dismissed from his office for subornation of forgery in connection with the prosecution of the famous Democratic leader Benedict Waldeck.[29] He was now engaged in palming off on the German public a series of apocryphal works, half memoirs and half historical romances, which he alleged were written by an Englishman named "Sir John Retcliffe." They dealt with all the palpitating international political problems and events of the middle of the nineteenth century, from the Crimean War to the War of the Danish Duchies. In one of these romances, entitled "Biarritz,"[30] he touched on the economic question which had been opened in its most formidable shape by the foundation of Lassalle's Workingmen's Union and the publication, in the previous year, of Marx's "Das Kapital." This led him to a melodramatic Jewish interlude.

Two of his characters, a Jewish Social Democrat named Lasali and a scientific dreamer named Faust, overhear the proceedings of a secret assembly of the "Elect of Israel," held once in every century round the tomb of a mythical "Holy Rabbi" named Simeon ben Jehudah in the ancient Jewish cemetery at Prague. The conclave is pictured as engaged in the worship of the Golden Calf,[31] which, we are told, has been

---

[28] As a matter of fact, he was not the first worker in this field, though he was the first literary ancestor of Nilus. The idea of the dramatic treatment of a Jewish conspiracy against Christian Society was worked out by the Polish poet Krassinsky in his *Nie-Boska Komedya* ("The Undivine Comedy"), published in 1834. It differs in scope and detail from Goedsche. Its attack on the Jews was strongly censured by Adam Mickiewicz.

[29] *Meyer's Konversations-Lexikon* (1897), Vol. VII., *sub. voc.* Goedsche and Waldeck. *Stenographischer Bericht über die Verhandlungen in der Anklage gegen Dr. Waldeck* (Berlin, 1849).

[30] In four volumes, Berlin, 1868.

[31] It was a custom of some mediæval German Jews to place the "first fruits" of their cattle to grass in the cemeteries. This gave rise to a popular belief that the idolatrous cultus of the Golden Calf still lingered among them. (Schudt: *Jüdische Merckwürdigkeiten* (1714), Vol. II., p. 376.)

preserved as the profoundest mystery of the Jewish Cabala by which the Jews may eventually secure their domination over all the nations of the earth. The practical application of the principles of this cultus is discussed in a long series of cynical speeches, which are in close agreement with the hypotheses of Gougenot des Mousseaux and similar writers. The Jews are to work with gold and the Press for the subversion of Christianity, and they are to act as a universal disturbing and demoralising instrument, so that in the fulness of time they may establish the Jewish Universal Dominion on the ruins of Christian society. When on the stroke of midnight this uncanny conventicle breaks up, Lasali solemnly pledges himself to his friend Faust to fight the hideous materialism of his co-religionists with the ideals of Social Democracy.[32]

This was the *editio princeps* of a number of forged anti-Semitic documents, of which the Nilus Protocols are the latest redaction. They differ among themselves in detail, according to the varying stages of the evolution of the political and economic struggle, but in their broad lines they are constant to the original presentation of their case by Goedsche.

The first forgeries, in which Goedsche's avowed fiction was transformed into protocols or reports of alleged Jewish confessions, were produced early in the eighties by the more irresponsible elements of the German anti-Semitic movement then in process of formation by Treitschke and Stöcker in Germany, and were widely circulated as broadsheets. In 1893 the same material was worked up simultaneously by two German anti-Semitic papers, the *Deutsch-soziale Blätter* and the *Antisemitische Korrespondenz*, and published as an authentic speech delivered by a Jewish Rabbi at a secret meeting of his

---

[32] *Biarritz*, Vol. I., pp. 130-180. Further characteristic references to the Jewish question will be found in a later novel of the Retcliffe series entitled *Um die Weltherrschaft*, Vol. I., pp. 309-310, 338, 360, 415; Vol. II., pp. 55, 56, 63; Vol. III., pp. 127, 130; Vol. IV., pp. 190-191, 467; Vol. V., pp. 22, 83-84, 206.

disciples held in the Jewish cemetery at Prague.[33] The source of this fabrication was placed beyond doubt by a thoughtless editorial statement that it was extracted from a work written by an eminent Englishman named "Sir John Retcliffe," and entitled "Memoirs of the Politico-Historical Events of the Last Ten Years." Needless to say, this book is as apocryphal as Retcliffe himself, the alleged speech being chiefly a condensed paraphrase of Goedsche's avowed fiction. There is, however, one important deviation from the original which brings it nearer to the Nilus text, the Jews being pictured not as divided into anti-Christian Materialists and Socialists, but as being all simulators of Socialism and Anarchism for their own revolutionary purposes while still remaining, among themselves, devotees of the Golden Calf, with all its moral, or rather immoral, implications. In 1901 a literal Czech translation of this precious protocol, but without the acknowledgment of indebtedness to "Retcliffe," was published in Prague under the title "A Rabbi on the Goyim."[34] It was immediately confiscated by the police on the ground that it was calculated to disturb the peace, but the anti-Semites revenged themselves by incorporating the whole text in an interpellation to the Minister of Justice, which was brought forward by the deputy Brzenovsky in the Austrian Reichsrath on March 13, 1901, and gave rise to a lively debate.[35] It was not heard of again until 1911, when it was translated into French—this time with the "Retcliffe" acknowledgment—by M. Kalixt de Wolski, and published together with a *réchauffé* of the more notorious forgeries of Braafmann and Lutostansky.[36] Finally, in 1912 the anti-Semitic Press in Germany republished it in a new form. Instead of an alleged historical document, it now appeared as a piece of news—a stenographic report of a speech delivered by a

---

[33] *Berichte über die 3 Generalversammlung des Vereins zur Abwehr des Antisemitismus* (Vienna, 1893), pp. 8, 9.

[34] Hebrew for "Gentiles."

[35] *Stenographische Protokolle des Hauses der Abgeordneten des Oesterreichischen Reichsrathes* (1901), pp. 1282-1284.

[36] Wolski: *La Russie Juive* (Paris, 1911), pp. 7-19.

"Jewish Rabbi" at a Jewish Congress held at Lemberg.[37] Anyone who takes the trouble, however, to make the comparison will find that it is a textual *précis* of the speeches made by the Golden Calf worshippers in Goedsche's "Biarritz."

It is consoling to note that none of these scandalous fabrications made any durable appeal to the relatively sober mentality of those happy pre-war days. No reputable newspaper noticed them. Even M. Drumont, while appropriating all the theories of Gougenot des Mousseaux in his "France Juive"—without acknowledgment, by the way—does not mention Goedsche or any of his malicious plunderers.

Now it needs but a very cursory glance at these forgeries and their raw material in the treatises of the literary scaremongers to perceive at once the fraud which has been practised on the public by Nilus's book. But before I press this point home, let us see whether Nilus himself has any reasonable explanation to offer of the *provenance* of his documents. It should be borne in mind that these documents consist of a number of so-called "Protocols of the Learned Elders of Zion," in which, as in the Goedsche romance, certain Jewish teachers are made to avow to their disciples the dark designs of Jewry for the corruption and subjugation of Christendom. Nilus does not refuse to say how he came by these Protocols. On the contrary he gives us no fewer than three explanations. Unfortunately for him, they are not only elusive and incredibly melodramatic, but they are also hopelessly contradictory. Two of them will be found in the English edition. According to one, the Protocols came from a deceased friend unnamed, who received them from a woman, also unnamed, who stole them from "one of the most influential and most highly initiated leaders of Freemasonry ... at the close of a secret meeting of the initiated in France."[38] According to the other, there was no woman intermediary and no despoiled French Freemason, but the whole business was done by the deceased friend himself, who rifled the safes of "the Headquarter Offices of the Society of

---

[37] The text is quoted by Meister: *Judas Schuldbuch*, p. 155.
[38] "The Jewish Peril," p. III.

Zion in France."[39] The inconsistency of these two stories may conceivably be explained, but it is not so easy to account for the third story, which Nilus relates in a third and enlarged edition of his work published in 1911. Here he tells us that the documents came not from France, but from Switzerland, that they were not Judeo-Masonic, but Zionist, and that they were the secret Protocols of the Zionist Congress held in Basle in 1897.[40] From these conflicting statements it is perfectly clear that Nilus is not a witness of truth, and the damaging conclusion suggested by a comparison of his Protocols with the Goedsche fiction and its progeny of forgeries becomes irresistible.

The Protocols are, in short, an amplified imitation of Goedsche's handiwork adapted to the circumstances of the Russian Revolution of 1905. Whether it was made direct from the melodramatic text of "Biarritz" is doubtful. Had Nilus worked with that document his credulous mysticism would assuredly not have resisted its Golden Calf theory, of which he is refreshingly innocent. On the other hand, he does adopt the blending of the Materialist and Social Democratic elements which are separate and conflicting in Goedsche, but which, with the exclusion of the Golden Calf, were the chief points of difference between the Czech forgery of 1901 and its Goedsche original. It therefore seems probable that it was with the Czech text that Nilus operated, and this is confirmed by his own avowal that the "manuscript" which first made him acquainted with the alleged Protocols was given to him in 1901, the year in which the Czech pamphlet was published.[41]

---

[39] *Ibid.*, p. 88.
[40] *Berliner Tageblatt*, May 18, 1920. The story is repeated with further variations, in the fourth edition, published in 1917, extracts from which are given in the *Morning Post*, August 12, 1920. In this edition Nilus quotes certain enigmatic statements of the late Theodor Herzl as proof of a secret Jewish teaching. It happens that the correspondence with Herzl on this subject is in the possession of the present writer. It has nothing to do with a secret Jewish teaching.
[41] Fourth edit., cap. III. (Quoted by *Morning Post*, Aug. 12, 1920.)

In his main ideas Nilus followed this pamphlet very closely, but borrows, or, rather, purloins, additional matter, especially in regard to the Freemasons, from Gougenot des Mousseaux. He also annexes political and economic ideas on a large scale from modern Russian reactionary writers and from certain early Bolshevist programme-mongers. How closely his main thesis follows that of the Czech-Goedsche pamphlet is shown by the following parallel, in which both explain how the Jews hope to accomplish their fell purpose by simulating sympathy with the proletariat and leading it into destructive, and eventually suicidal, political revolution:—

THE CZECH GOEDSCHE.

"Our people are conservative, faithful to the religious ceremonies and customs which have been bequeathed to us by our ancestors, but our interest exacts that we should simulate a zeal for the social questions which are the order of the day, especially those which deal with the amelioration of the condition of workmen. In reality our efforts should be directed to capturing this movement of public opinion. The blindness of the masses, their propensity to yield themselves to oratory as empty as it is sonorous, makes of them an easy prey and a docile instrument of popularity and credit. We shall find without difficulty among our own

NILUS.

"We intend to appear as though we were the liberators of the labouring man come to free him from his oppression, when we shall suggest to him to join the ranks of our armies of socialists, anarchists, and communists.... We govern the masses by making use of feelings of jealousy and hatred kindled by oppression and need.... When the time comes for our Worldly Ruler to be crowned we will see to it that by the same means—that is to say, by making use of the people the expression of such factitious sentiments and as much eloquence as sincere Christians find in their enthusiasm. We must as much as possible sustain the proletariat and bring it within the reach of those who have money at their disposal. By this means we shall be able to rouse the masses whenever we please, to lead them into upheavals and revolutions. Each of these catastrophes will advance by a long stride our own racial interests and will rapidly bring us nearer to our one great end—that of reigning over all the earth as it has been promised to us by our Father Abraham." mob—we will destroy everything that may prove to be an obstacle in our way.... The populace in its ignorance blindly believes in printed words and in erroneous delusions which have been duly inspired by us.... The mob is used to listen to us who pay it for its attention and obedience. By these means we shall create such a blind force that it will never be capable of taking any decision without the guidance of our agents placed by us for the purpose of leading them".[42]

It would be easy to quote many other equally deadly parallels, but this one will assuredly suffice to show that, in their main argument, at any rate, the Protocols are not what they pretend to be—that is an actual statement of secret Jewish teaching by a Jew—but that they are not even an echo of Jewish ideas, seeing that they are derived from a Gentile forgery based on a work of confessedly Gentile imagination.

When we examine Nilus's added matter the revelation of fraud becomes still more remarkable. The main difference between Nilus and his German and Czech fore-runners is that he works out in detail the alleged Autocratic and Bolshevist

---

[42] "The Jewish Peril," pp. 12, 13, 14, 32.

philosophy of his Elders of Zion. He pictures these fabulous personages as genuine believers in Autocracy, but more intent on Jewish political domination than on merely mercenary exploitation. Accordingly, he attributes to them the design of practising a sort of State Bolshevism when their domination shall have been accomplished—that is to say, the creation of a paternal Jewish autocracy basing itself on a carefully controlled communistic system. It is by this ingenious device that he endeavours to show that the Jews are the arch-enemy at both extremes of the social organism.

Now, whence comes the autocratic philosophy he puts into the mouths of his Jewish Elders? It is exclusively a Russian doctrine. Nilus knows this very well, and he does not waste time in the hopeless task of finding counterblasts to democracy in Jewish political literature. He goes straight to the fountain-head of Russian obscurantism in the person of the late Procurator of the Holy Synod, Konstantine Petrovich Pobyedonoszeff! This expedient has the appearance almost of a practical joke, for Pobyedonoszeff was not only a pure Muscovite and a fanatical Greek Christian, but so conspicuous an anti-Semite and oppressor of Jews, Stundists, and other Russian allogenes that he earned for himself the sobriquet of "the modern Torquemada." Nilus's Jewish Antichrist is, in short, nothing more than the austere super-Christian Procurator masquerading, like Edward Alleyn's Barabas, in a false nose and a prodigious property beard.

The evidence of this jumps to the eyes if we take the trouble to compare the first part of "The Jewish Peril" with Mr. Robert Crozier Long's translation of Pobyedonoszeff's "Reflections of a Russian Statesman,"[43] especially the chapters on "The New Democracy" and "The Great Falsehood of our Time." Many parallel passages might be quoted, but it will, perhaps, suffice if I extract one, fundamental to both writers, in which Nilus makes the Jewish Elder plagiarise the argument of the Christian Procurator, in part almost textually:—

---

[43] Lond., 1898.

POBYEDONOSZEFF.

"Forever extending its base, the new Democracy now aspires to universal suffrage. By this means, *the political power would be shattered into a number of infinitesimal bits, of which each citizen acquires a single one.* What will he do with it then; how will he employ it?... *Each vote representing an inconsiderable fragment of power, by itself signifies nothing....* The extension of the right to participate in elections is regarded as progress, and as the conquest of freedom by democratic theorists who hold that the more numerous the participants in political rights, the greater is the probability that all will employ this right in the interests of the public welfare. Experience proves a very different thing. The history of mankind bears witness that the most necessary and fruitful reforms emanated from the supreme will of statesmen or from a minority enlightened by lofty ideas and deep knowledge, and that, on the contrary, the extension of the representative

NILUS.

"It suffices to give the populace self-government for a short period for this populace to become a disorganised rabble.... Is it possible for the mass to discriminate quietly and without jealousies to administer the affairs of State? Can they be a defence against a foreign foe? This is impossible, *as a plan broken up into as many parts as there are minds in the mass loses its value, and therefore becomes unintelligible and unworkable.* Alone an autocrat can conceive vast plans clearly, assigning its proper part to everything in the mechanism of the machine of State. Hence we conclude that it is expedient for the welfare of the country that the Government of the same should be in the hands of one responsible person. Without absolute despotism civilisation cannot exist, for civilisation

principle is accompanied by an abasement of political ideas".[44]

is capable of being promoted only under the protection of the ruler, whoever he may be, and not at the hands of the masses".[45]

In the second part of "The Jewish Peril," where the Elders of Zion are made to expound their State Bolshevism, the sources are not quite so clear. It is practically certain, however, that they are not Jewish. Had Nilus waited a few years he would, perhaps, have been able to quote convinced Bolshevist writers of Jewish birth like Radek and Zinovieff, but when he wrote in 1905 there were no such exponents of pure Leninism. The great split of 1903 found all the leading Russo-Jewish Socialists, such as Martoff, Axelrod, Trotsky, Martinoff, Liber, Dahn, and the whole of the Bund, ranged with the Mensheviks against Lenin.[46] The result was that, in reproducing Bolshevist ideas, Nilus must have been dependent on Gentile pamphleteers. It is not easy to identify these ephemeral writings with certainty, but many interesting parallels of this section of the Protocols may be found in Bucharin's "Programme of the Communists," which codifies all the early Bolshevist literature.[47] And Bucharin, be it noted, is just as little a Jew as was Pobyedonoszeff. This, of course, explains the alleged prophetic character of the Protocols which the *Morning Post* and its friends hold to be convincing evidence of their genuineness. If the Bolsheviks have acted on some of the

---

[44] Pobyedonoszeff: "Reflections" (English edit.), pp. 26, 27, 28. Allowance must be made for the different styles and qualities of the two translations.

[45] "The Jewish Peril," pp. 2, 5.

[46] Mautner: *Der Bolschewismus* (Stuttgart, 1920), p. 95. See also Landau-Aldanov: *Lenine* (Paris, 1920), pp. 31-32. It is amusing to note that the *Morning Post* (July 21, 1920) counts almost all these Jewish Mensheviks as Bolsheviks.

[47] The date of the original Russian edition is unknown to the present writer, but a German edition was published at Zurich in 1918.

principles attributed the Elders of Zion, they have done so not because they were of Jewish origin, but because they were exclusively the work of Lenin and his bodyguard of Gentile proletarians.

So much for the literary history of the Protocols. Their political history is not less discreditable. They were not published because they were discovered—whether in the pages of Goedsche or elsewhere—but they were discovered because they were wanted for the ignoble purpose of a pogrom-weapon. In the first edition of his book, published in 1901, Nilus knew nothing of them, but was absorbed by the more abstract aspects of the problem of Antichrist. In 1905 occurred the Russian Revolution, and this was followed by the incendiary conspiracy of the Okhrana to stir up pogroms all over Russia and drown the new Constitution in a welter of Jewish blood.[48] Nilus appears to have been employed by the Okhrana in this wicked campaign. At any rate, the Protocols first appeared at this date in the shape of small pamphlets or broadsheets and they were only afterwards collected and incorporated in a second edition of Nilus's work as a *dénouement* of his theory of the Judeo-Masonic nature of Antichrist. Nor has their *rôle* as a pogrom-weapon been confined to the year 1905. Quite recently abstracts of them were widely circulated in Denikin's and Koltchak's armies. They were printed in the Eparchial Library at Rostoff, and were distributed by the remnants of the organisation of Black Hundreds known as the Union of the Russian People. How effective they were for their murderous purpose we know from the horrible massacres of inoffensive Jews and Jewesses which dogged the foot-steps of Denikin's armies throughout South Russia.

But this was not the only sinister movement with which the Protocols seem to have been associated. The year in which they were first published in Russia was also the year of a very serious Russo-German intrigue against the Triple Entente; and here again these Protocols—or, rather, their argument—appear as one of the main weapons of the plotters.

---

[48] Séménoff: "The Russian Government and the Massacres" (Lond., 1907).

It will be remembered that in July, 1905, the basis of an anti-British Alliance was secretly agreed upon by the Tsar and the Kaiser at Bjoerkoe.[49] A few months later, while the Treaty was still incomplete, Count Lamsdorf proposed to the Tsar that advantage should be taken of "the new friendly relations" with Germany to conclude an agreement between the two countries for combating the alleged Jewish and Masonic peril.[50] Now, the secret Memorandum in which this precious scheme was set forth, and which the Tsar formally approved in January, 1906, is virtually a reproduction of the anti-Semitic argument which the alleged "Protocols of the Elders of Zion" are designed to prove. It is true that the Protocols themselves are not mentioned, but Count Lamsdorf is none the less positive, with the fabricators of those documents, that the Jews are the soul of the Revolutionary movement in Europe, that their "principal aim is the all-around triumph of anti-Christian and anti-Monarchist Jewry," that their millionaires subvention this movement with "gigantic pecuniary means," and that they are abetted in this enterprise by the Freemasons. The Protocols are, indeed, little more than a dramatic version of Count Lamsdorf's Memorandum. It is difficult to resist the conclusion that in some occult way— perhaps not so very occult—Nilus's book was intended to serve the sinister ends of the pro-German foreign policy of Count Lamsdorf in the same way as it served the bloody purposes of the pogrom-mongers. It should be especially noted in this connection that the book is as anti-British as it is anti-Jewish, and that it was published in December, 1905, that is to say, at the very time that the Tsar had the Lamsdorf scheme under consideration.

The more recent history of the Protocols is even more unsavoury. It is incredible, but it is nevertheless a fact, that these

---

[49] "The Nikky-Willy Correspondence," *Times*, Sept. 4, 1917; *Daily Telegraph*, Sept. 4, 27, and 29, 1917; and *Morning Post*, Sept. 15, 1917.

[50] For Russian text of Count Lamsdorf's proposal see Vol. VI. of "Secret Documents," published by the Soviet Commissariat of Foreign Affairs. An English translation with an introduction appears in Wolf: "Diplomatic History of the Jewish Question" (London, 1919), pp. 54-62.

crazy forgeries have played a part behind the scenes in the international combinations for assisting the anti-Bolshevist reaction in Russia, which have filled so much of the public mind during the last two years, and which have cost this country close on £100,000,000. There was a moment when the Great Powers were disposed to leave the Russians to fight out their quarrels among themselves. Various objections to this policy were urged by the friends of Admiral Koltchak and General Denikin, and among them was the argument that there was, in fact, no civil war in Russia, that Bolshevism was not Russian, but exclusively alien, the work of international Jews who were themselves the instruments of a world-wide and deep-laid Jewish conspiracy against Christendom and the political order of Europe. Bolshevism was, in short, a European menace. Russia was pictured as the first instalment of the Jewish conquest of Europe, which had already sent its *éclaireurs* to Berlin, Dresden, Vienna, and Budapest, whence they were advancing to the Rhine and the Alps. In support of this argument, Russian Intelligence Officers, armed with doctored typewritten translations of the Nilus Protocols, with the anti-British passages carefully expunged, were sent to London, Paris, Rome, and Washington, where they circulated this precious literature confidentially among Cabinet Ministers, heads of public departments, and persons of influence in society and journalism. That this campaign was not fruitless is attested by many curious facts, which, unfortunately, cannot be more particularly referred to at this moment without a breach of confidence. Overt evidence of the mischief that was wrought is, however, not wanting. It may be found, for example, in certain oracular utterances of Mr. Winston Churchill in a Sunday paper, in the anti-Semitic outbursts of the *Morning Post,* and the itching of the *Times* and the *Spectator* to do likewise, and, finally, in the discreditable propaganda leaflets distributed in the interior of Russia by the air service of the British armies at Archangel and Murmansk.[51]

---

[51] These leaflets were very promptly withdrawn as soon as the attention of His Majesty's Government was called to them.

Why the Protocols were circulated thus secretly is clear. Their political purpose had nothing to gain, and, indeed, everything to lose from public criticism and discussion. Nevertheless, they leaked out. A copy got into the hands of an official of the United States Department of Justice, and he, anxious for further information, and following some tactless office rule, sent it to the President of an important Jewish organisation in New York for his observations. The President promptly replied that it was a forgery of a very familiar type, and took no further notice of it. In June, 1919, the present writer, while in Paris, heard of the circulation of the Protocols as a pogrom pamphlet in Denikin's country, but he also attached no special importance to it. Later on came the first intimation of the proposed publication of the Protocols in Western Europe. It came in very characteristic shape. One day the members of a certain Jewish Delegation in Paris received a visit from a mysterious Lithuanian who had been connected with the Russian Secret Police. He professed himself anxious to serve the Jewish community, and said that he was in a position to prevent the publication of an exceedingly dangerous book, which, if it saw the light, would probably involve the whole house of Israel in ruin. Quite naturally, he wished to be paid for this service, but the sum was a mere trifle, a matter of £10,000. He was asked for a sight of the volume, and he produced it. It was, of course, "the Protocols." Needless to say, no business was done. It was possibly only a coincidence that in the following December a German edition was published under the title "Die Geheimnisse der Weisen von Zion," and two months later the English edition saw the light under the title "The Jewish Peril: Protocols of the Learned Elders of Zion." The German and English publication would have been simultaneous but for the fact that difficulty was experienced in finding a reputable London publishing house to take the Protocols seriously.

One further word about the English edition. Its history and aims are much less clear than those of its Russian original, owing partly to the circumspect anonymity in which its sponsors have elected to veil themselves. It is inconceivable that it is intended to stir up pogroms in this country, though the suggestion is not obscurely made in recent articles in the *Times* and the *Spectator*. More probably—as has already been hinted—it is part of a German intrigue to prejudice the recent German general elections in favour of the Militarist Reactionaries and perhaps even to justify the forcible upsetting of the German Government by means of another Kapp *Putsch*. Here is the evidence for this startling conjecture.

The German Reactionaries have lately been putting all their money on anti-Semitism. Their publicity agencies in Charlottenburg and Munich have flooded the country with pamphlets denouncing the Republican Government as a Judaized Junta, the instrument of a far-reaching Judeo-Masonic conspiracy to ruin Germany and to involve the whole of Christian and Monarchical Europe in her fate. This campaign has lately become official, and a paragraph was inserted in the Electoral Manifesto of the German Nationalists—the party of Kapp and Lutzow—formally adopting anti-Semitism as a plank in their platform. One of the aims of the party is to secure foreign sympathy and help, and they hope to do this by finding a common ground in anti-Semitism. In these circumstances the publication of "The Jewish Peril" in England wears a disturbing significance, but it becomes much more disturbing when we find that the German edition was published almost simultaneously with it, with a dedication appealing not only to the German people, but also to "The Princes of Europe." The object was clearly to get English support, and unfortunately the response was not long in coming. On May 8th the *Times* was inveigled into publishing an article expressing alarm at the revelations of the Protocols and calling for an investigation. The delight of the German Reactionaries knew no bounds. It was voiced by Count Reventlow in a long article in the *Deutsche Tageszeitung* of May 17 welcoming the *Times's* acceptance of the Jewish peril as an indication that English public opinion was beginning to recognise the righteousness of Kapp and Co. in their resistance to the Ebert *régime* and what the Count called the "pax Judaeica."[52]

Whether the translators and editors of "The Jewish Peril" have consciously lent themselves to this intrigue, which is part of the German Reactionary plot to upset the Treaty of Versailles and perhaps plunge Europe into another war, cannot be said. But assuredly the worst suspicions are permissible so long as these gentlemen elect to skulk in the *coulisses* and shrink from responsibility for their scrubby handiwork. Even Titus Oates had the courage of his forgeries.

---

[52] Besides Count Reventlow's article see a very light-giving article entitled "Reventlow und die Weisen von Zion" in the *Berliner Tageblatt*, May 18, 1920.

III
JEWS AND BOLSHEVISM

The final argument of the anti-Semitic scaremongers is the Judeo-Bolshevik bogey. The *Morning Post* theory of "World Unrest" may prove difficult of assimilation to matter-of-fact minds, and the authenticity of the Nilus Protocols may be suspect, but the Bolshevism of the Jews is asserted to be an incontrovertible fact, which proves that both the theory and its documents are morally justifiable. Were it not for its very tragical possibilities, the evocation of this bogey would be a fit subject for mirth, or, at best, a problem for the folk-lorist or the student of corporate hallucination. As it is, it is a very serious matter, seeing that the lives of many thousands of innocent persons are jeopardised by it.

The bogey takes the specific form of a charge against the Jews of Russia and Poland that they are for the most part Bolsheviks, and that the Bolshevist revolution was engineered by them and is still controlled and directed by them.[53] The only evidence cited in support of it is that Trotsky and a few of the more prominent Bolshevist commissaries are men of Jewish birth, and that a similar element on an even more restricted scale is found in certain of the Soviets. But those men are no more Jews than Lenin, Lunacharsky, Chicherin, and the great bulk of the Russian Bolsheviks are Christians. It would, indeed, be just as reasonable to say that the mainstay of Russian Bolshevism is to be found in American and British Christendom because it has found sympathisers in Mr. Bullitt and Mr. Steffens, in Mr. Goode, Mr. Price, Mr. Russell, Mr. Ransome, Mr. Hunt, and many other Americans and Englishmen of Christian birth.

The appearance of the bogey at this moment is not difficult to understand. There has always been at the back of the anti-

---

[53] *Morning Post* articles on "The Cause of World Unrest," *passim.* See particularly July 21, 1920.

Semitic mind an uneasy feeling that the Jews are, as the old law books say, *perpetui inimici Regis et Religionis*. Their participation in the bourgeois Revolutions of 1830 and 1848 gave political point to this superstition, and ever since it has been a favourite theory of the more fanatical reactionaries that the whole Democratic movement in Europe is a Jewish conspiracy for the subversion of Christianity and Christian society. In this respect the *Morning Post* theory is, as has already been shown, not new. In Russia it became early an expedient of reactionary tactics. To denounce revolution on its merits was difficult, but to denounce it as a Jewish conspiracy against the Throne and the Altar was always calculated to impress large classes of the population who otherwise might not have been indisposed to look indulgently on a great political change. This was the cue of all the incendiary appeals of the Okhrana against the Revolution of 1905.[54]

Thus, when Bolshevism arose, it was quite in the line of traditional Russian policy to denounce it as the work of the Jews. From the reactionary camps of Deniken and Koltchak, and even from the Allied armies in the North, where the Intelligence and Propaganda Services were necessarily in the hands of Russian officers of the old Tsarist *régime*, the country was flooded with pamphlets and broadsheets declaring that Bolshevism was a Jewish plot, and that the aim of those who were making war on it was not to fight their Russian brothers, but to deliver them from their Jewish bondage. It was, however, in Germany that the bogey was adapted for consumption in Western Europe. The old Junker anti-Semitism received a great impulse from the collapse of thrones which followed the Armistice of 1918. All the revolutionary movements were at once attributed by them to the Jews, and, by way of showing the victorious Allies the danger they were courting by tolerating them, bloodcurdling pictures of Russian Bolshevism as the first fruits of an international Jewish conspiracy were issued from the presses of the anti-Semitic

---

[54] Séménoff, *op. cit.*

43

society known as *Deutschland's Erneuerung*, in Munich.[55] A circle of Russian Monarchist refugees in Berlin founded a weekly paper called *The Sunbeam* to help in the holy work. It was in the columns of this journal that translations of extracts from Nilus's forged Protocols first appeared.[56] Early in 1919 the themes of these imbecile ephemerides were gathered up and co-ordinated in bulky volumes by Baron Hans von Liebig,[57] by Dr. Friedrich Wichtl, and by a person calling himself "Wilhelm Meister."[58] These writers were the final artificers of the bogey as we now know it, Trotsky being represented in their pages as the conscious instrument not only of the Jewish Rabbinate and of Jewish finance, but also of the secretly Judaised Masonic Lodges. A curious restatement of this apocalypse will be found in an anonymous pamphlet, entitled "Le Bolshevisme," which was printed in Paris last year by the Jesuits of the Rue Garancière.[59] The French, however, have been very loth to touch this unclean product of German *Kultur*.

We need only glance at the leading tenets of the Bolsheviks to realise how stupid all this is—indeed, how impossible it is that Bolshevism should find even an appreciable measure of sympathy in the Jewish community. Lenin, Trotsky, and their associates are not only extreme Communists, but are also avowed Atheists. On the other hand, the great bulk of the Jews of Russia are extremely orthodox members of the Synagogue, who hold in horror every symptom of Atheism. The strength of this element was recently estimated by M. Paderewski himself at 75 per cent. In their economic affiliation these Jews are not less hostile to Bolshevism. They belong in an overwhelming proportion to the upper and middle-class bourgeoisie. Moreover, the Jew is instinctively and

---

[55] The chief members of this Society, which is as Anglophobe as it is Judeophobe, are a brother of General Von Below and the renegade Houston Stewart Chamberlain.

[56] S. Poliakoff in *La Tribune Juive* (Paris), No. 21.

[57] *Der Betrug am Deutschen Volke* (Munich, 1919).

[58] *Supra*, p. 6.

[59] It provoked an excellent reply by "Un Russe" entitled *Bolchevisme et Judaïsme* (Paris, 1919).

by all his traditions an individualist. It has been possible to found under the great names of Lamennais, Kingsley, Maurice, Hughes, Bishop Ketteler, and others a school of Christian Communism seeking its sanctions in the teachings of orthodox Christianity. No such school in the strictly economic sense exists or is possible in the Jewish Church. Marx and Lassalle ceased to be Jews long before they became Socialists, and, in so far as the Jewish proletariat which has arisen in Russia and Poland under the stress of exceptional and ephemeral conditions is Socialistic, it is notoriously remote from the Synagogue—as from every other kind of "clericalism"—and impatient of its control.

But, it is said, the Jews must be held responsible for Bolshevism because Bolshevism is only applied Marxism, and Marx was a Jew. I have already pointed out that, strictly speaking, Marx was not a Jew, but, even supposing he were, that would not make Bolshevism a Jewish creation, seeing that in point of fact it is, in its main lines, not even Marxist. There is so much loose thinking on this question that it may be well to indicate—however briefly—the fundamental differences between the teachings of Marx and Lenin. In the first place, Marx was a Democrat, while Lenin is confessedly an Oligarch. Democracy is axiomatic with Marx, the foundation of all his doctrine. Lenin, on the other hand, derides the mere counting of heads. He is, as he would put it, for the supremacy of truth, whatever the number of its disciples. This vital difference affects the systems of the two men at all essential points. Thus, while Marx teaches that the Dictatorship of the Proletariat should be the outcome of a Democratic Republic based on Universal Suffrage, Lenin rejects Universal Suffrage, and bases the Dictatorship on a Guild or Soviet Republic. Again, Marx stands for Revolution by Law in all Democratic States, while Lenin stands for Revolution by Force, whatever the constitution of the State. Nor does this apply only to revolutions, for while Marx holds that the authority of the State must, whenever possible, be exercised by peaceful means, Lenin teaches that Force is inherent in the State and its exercise unavoidable. This leads Lenin to the view of Robespierre that even the Terror is in a sense mystically sanctified—a view of which Marx never dreamt in his most daring moments. Finally, contrast the conceptions of the State as set forth by the two men. Both, of course, are for the State, but while Marx pictures it, after the decision of the Class War, as composed of the whole Democracy seeking the conciliation of its conflicting elements, Lenin would confine it to the Dictatorship of the Proletariat, even though the other classes might be in the majority.[60] There is, of course, much to be said for both theories within the ring-fence of Socialist polemics, but I am not concerned at this moment with their respective merits. All I want to show is that Marx cannot be held responsible for Bolshevism as we know it, and that if the alleged Jewishness of Bolshevism rests on the theory that it has any essential affinity with Marxism it is singularly unconvincing.

The case against the bogey is, however, not limited to these generalisations. It may be said, while the upper and middle classes in Jewry are probably free from Bolshevism, this is not the case with the Jewish proletariat. If not orthodox Jews, they certainly profess a strong Jewish nationalism, and if from them Bolshevism draws its main strength, then Jewry must bear the responsibility. On this point, happily, very definite information is available. First, with regard to the leaders. Bolshevism was founded in 1903, through a split among the Russian Socialists, which took the form of a revolt against Lenin. Who led the revolt? The Jew Martoff, and he was supported by all the most conspicuous Jews in the party, including Trotsky himself.[61] They were followed by the great bulk of the rank-and-file of so-called Jewish Socialists. How true this is, can be shown by an analysis of the Leninite party fourteen years later. In the autumn of 1917 the Bolsheviks themselves published a statistical analysis of the constituents of the Soviets, with special regard to their geographical and ethnographical distribution. It was there shown that the

---

[60] See on this subject the elaborate analysis of the two teachings in Mautner, *op. cit.*, pp. 120-296.

[61] Mautner (p. 95) and Landau-Aldanov (pp. 31-32), *op. cit.*

Bolsheviks had a clear majority over the Mensheviks, or non-Bolshevist Socialists, and that they were far more largely composed of pure Russian elements than the Mensheviks. Their greatest strength was found in the districts of Petrograd, Moscow, the Baltic Provinces, the Volga, the Ural, and Asiatic Russia, where the Great-Russian working masses dominate. On the other hand, the Mensheviks were almost entirely confined to the western and south-western provinces, the Don district, and the Caucasus, where the chief non-Russian races are found. Here the return for the Jewish Pale of Settlement that is, the provinces in which 95 per cent. of the Jews of Russia and Poland reside—is most significant. The number of organised Mensheviks is given at 18,000, while of organised Bolsheviks there is no trace whatever in the whole region. The other non-Russian districts in these provinces were less fortunate, for in the south-western governments the proportion of Bolsheviks to Mensheviks was 8 to 11, in the Don district 18 to 29, and in the Caucasus 1 to 5. The statistics here, however, show clearly that the strength of Bolshevism was always in an inverse ratio to the strength of the local Jewish population.[62]

Another important piece of evidence is to be found in the attitude of the Jewish "Bund," which is the main organisation of Jewish workmen in Poland and the Pale of Settlement. From the beginning of the Russian Revolution the "Bund," avowedly Socialist, threw all its strength on the side of the Mensheviks. The most passionate struggles in the Congress of Soviets in 1917 were those waged between Lenin, on behalf of the Bolsheviks, and Liber, the "Bund" leader, on behalf of the Mensheviks. Liber and his colleague Dahn were at that time among the staunchest supporters of the policy of the Entente in Russia. To this day the great majority of the members of the "Bund" have remained anti-Bolshevist in doctrine, although under the pressure of the administration and for other political reasons which have appealed equally to many ex-Tsarist generals and Christian

---

[62] Report of the Commissar for National Economy reprinted from the *Novaya Shisn* in the *Bote* (Stockholm), Dec. 6, 1917.

Conservatives, they have lately pledged their allegiance to the Lenin *régime*. In political thought they are still numbered among the most ardent supporters of the great coalition of Russian Mensheviks, which has its headquarters in Stockholm, and—another significant fact—is captained by a Jew, the well-known Socialist writer Paul Axelrod. There are probably quite as many Jewish leaders in the anti-Bolshevist coalition as there are Jewish Commissaries among the Bolsheviks.

Nor are the upper and middle-classes of Russian and Polish Jewry merely passive spectators of the struggle. Politically they belong in an overwhelming proportion to the moderate Liberal party known as the Cadets, and many of them are active in the councils and Press of that party. The present leader of the Cadets, who succeeded Professor Miliukoff, after his unhappy but temporary defection from the cause of the Entente, is the distinguished Jewish lawyer M. Vinaver, equally conspicuous for his devotion to his co-religionists and the cause of ordered liberty in Russia. Admiral Koltchak and General Denikin, in spite of their compromising anti-Semitic associates, had no more strenuous supporter and no wiser counsellor than M. Vinaver. Another eminent Jew who may frequently be seen in consultation with MM. Sazonoff and Maklakoff at the Russian Delegation in Paris is Baron Alexandre de Gunzburg, at one time the most conspicuous member of the Jewish Community in Petrograd.

The anti-Semitic impression that Bolshevism is largely Jewish is, however, not altogether a bad dream, but rather an optical delusion which has been maliciously exaggerated. The so-called Jewish Bolsheviks are, indeed, a corps of officers without an army, and the anti-Semites have a little too hastily inferred the army. Even then these officers are not of the first rank. We have heard a great deal of "Jewish Commissars," and I find a notorious German anti-Semitic book quoting Mr. Robert Wilton, of the *Times*, as its authority for the statement that "of 384 People's Commissars who constitute the Government only 13 are Russians, while 300 are Jews."[63] What are the facts? The only

---

[63] Meister, *op. cit.*, p. 192.

officials in Soviet Russia who are authorised to hold the rank of People's Commissars are the members of the Cabinet.[64] These number 17,[65] and of them 16 are indisputably Gentiles, while only one—Trotsky—is of Jewish birth. And Trotsky, be it remembered, is a Jew who has publicly abjured the Jewish and all other religions, and who is so little a Jew in other respects that at the Socialist Congresses at the beginning of the century he led the cosmopolitans in denunciation of the Jewish Nationalism of the Bund. To describe Russian Bolshevism as Jewish because one member of Lenin's Council of People's Commissars is an apostate Jew is obviously ludicrous. Lenin might far more justly describe the anti-Bolshevism of Western Europe as Jewish because two years ago the French Cabinet contained one professing Jew and the British two. The other so-called Jewish Commissars are all men of the second and lower ranks of officials belonging exclusively either to the Civil Service or the Soviet analogue of our municipal life. They are probably fairly numerous, but in what may be called the second rank they do not number more than ten at the outside.[66] The others may or may not be convinced Bolsheviks. They are servants of the State who may have many other motives for serving the Soviets than an enthusiasm for Lenin's politics. Not every head of a Government Department or Chairman of a County Council in England is to-day necessarily a Lloyd Georgian. Trotsky has in his War Office and Corps of Officers probably as many ex-Tsarist officers—including sixteen Generals[67]—as there are "Jewish Commissars" in the whole Soviet Administration. And yet nobody dreams of describing the Red Legions as a Tsarist army. These officers are probably not even Bolsheviks. If we could know their motives we

---

[64] "Constitution of the Russian Soviet Republic," Article 48.

[65] *Ibid.*, Article 43.

[66] As the result of a careful analysis M. Poliakoff gives their names as follows: Zinovieff, Radek, Sverdloff, Steklof-Nakhamkes, Litvinoff, Larine, Kameneff, Ganetzki-Furstenberg, Joffe and Ounitzky. Of these two are dead and one is only a half-Jew (*La Tribune Juive*, Dec. 26, 1919).

[67] *Ibid.*, gives full list.

should probably find that they were not very widely different from those which actuate the "Jewish Commissars."

All this is not to say that there are no professing Jews in the Bolshevist ranks, or that the number of indifferent and apostate Jews who have thrown in their lot with the Soviets is quite negligible. What is contended is that normally the Jew is intensely anti-pathetic to Bolshevism, and that at the beginning of the Revolution relatively very few Jews—even of those who are Jews by race only—rallied to the call of Lenin. That this situation has changed during the last year is not improbable. But with whom does the blame rest? If Jews have reluctantly turned towards Bolshevism, it is because they have been forced into it by the anti-Bolsheviks. They cannot but be alarmed by the persistency and passion with which the charge of Bolshevism is levelled at them, and the threats which come from all sides to avenge in their persons the sins of Lenin and Trotsky. They have had a bloody instalment of this St. Bartholomew in the pogroms of the Polish borderlands and the Ukrainian plains. What wonder, then, if some of them—and they can only be relatively very few—turn for protection to the Soviets, especially in the lands where the Soviets rule? Nevertheless, their aversion from Bolshevism in theory and practice remains, and is, indeed, for the great majority of them insuperable.

One word in conclusion. If some of the charges against the Jews which have been examined in the foregoing pages were not so utterly unfounded as they prove to be, ample explanation and excuse might be found in the high and sustained tragedy of Jewish history. When in 1848 Ludwig Boerne was reproached by a political colleague with the excessiveness of his revolutionary zeal, he replied: "I was born a slave, and hence I love freedom better than you do." Twenty centuries of a terrible oppression has made of the Jews in Europe an element of no small importance in all the struggles for popular liberties, but throughout it all they have always remained a relatively conservative force. This is most strikingly exemplified by their career in the Russian Revolution. Human nature being what it is, it would not have been surprising if all the Jews in Russia had become fanatical Bolsheviks. The extravagances of Bolshevism are the natural reaction against the cruelties of Tsarism, and the Jews suffered more bitterly from those cruelties than any other section of the sorely tried Russian people. And yet their innate moderation—what Disraeli rightly diagnosed as their ineradicable attachment to Religion and Property—has prevailed, and even among the lower classes, who were proletariatised and driven to Socialism by the infamous May Laws,[68] Bolshevism has found only few and reluctant recruits. The Jews, no doubt, have their defects, very much in the same way as Christians, but what Mr. Gladstone once called "incivism" is not one of them.

---

[68] See Prof. A.V. Dicey's introduction to "The Legal Sufferings of the Jews in Russia" (Lond., 1912).

THE
PROTOCOLS
OF THE
LEARNED ELDERS
OF ZION

Excerpt from "THE LONDON TIMES",
Tuesday, August 16, 1921, pp. 9, 10

"JEWISH WORLD PLOT."

AN EXPOSURE.

THE SOURCE OF THE PROTOCOLS.

TRUTH AT LAST.

The so-called "Protocols of the Elders of Sion" were published in London last year under the title of "The Jewish Peril."

This book is a translation of a book published in Russia in 1905, by Sergei Nilus, a government official, who professed to have received from a friend a copy of a summary of the minutes of a secret meeting, held in Paris, by a Jewish organization that was plotting to overthrow civilization in order to establish a Jewish world state.

These "Protocols" attracted little attention until after the Russian Revolution of 1917, when the appearance of the Bolshevists, among whom were many Jews, professing and practicing political doctrines that in some points resembled those advocated in the "Protocols," led many to believe that Nilus' alleged discovery was genuine. The "Protocols" were widely discussed and translated into several European languages. Their authenticity has been frequently attacked and many arguments have been adduced for the theory that they are a forgery.

In the following articles our Constantinople Correspondent for the first time presents conclusive proof that the document is in the main a clumsy plagiarism. He has forwarded us a copy of the French book from which the plagiarism is made. The British Museum has a complete copy of the book, which is entitled, "Dialogue aux Enfers entre Machiavel et Montesquieu, ou la Politique de Machiavel au XIX. Siècle. Par un Contemporain," and was published at Brussels in 1865. Shortly after its publication the author, Maurice Joly, a Paris lawyer and publicist, was arrested by the police of Napoleon III. and sentenced to 18 months' imprisonment.

A LITERARY FORGERY.

(From Our Constantinople Correspondent.)

"There is one thing about Constantinople that is worth your while to remember," said a diplomatist to the writer in 1908. "If you only stay here long enough you will meet many men who matter, and you may find the key to many strange secrets." Yet I must confess that when the discovery which is the theme of these articles was communicated to me I was at first incredulous. Mr. X who brought me the evidence was convinced.

"Read this book through," he said, "and you will find irrefutable proof that the 'Protocols of the Learned Elders of Sion' is a plagiarism."

Mr. X., who does not wish his real name to be known, is a Russian landowner with English connexions. Orthodox by religion, he is in Political opinion a Constitutional Monarchist. He came here as a refugee after the final failure of the White cause in South Russia. He had long been interested in the Jewish question as far as it concerned Russia, had studied the "Protocols," and during the period of Denikin's ascendancy had made investigations with the object of discovering whether any occult "Masonic" organization, such as the "Protocols" speak of, existed in Southern Russia. The only such organization was a Monarchist one. The discovery of the key to the problem of the "Protocols" came to him by chance.

THE SWISS ORIGINAL.

A few months ago he bought a number of old books from a former officer of the "Okhrana" (Political Police) who had fled to Constantinople. Among these books was a small volume in French, lacking the title page, with dimensions of 5 ½ in. by 3 ¾ in. It had been cheaply rebound. On the leather back is printed in Latin capitals the word Joli. The preface, entitled "Simple avertissement," is dated Geneva, October 15, 1864. The book contains 324 pages, of which numbers 315-322 inclusive follow page 24 in the only copy known to Mr. X, perhaps owing to a mistake when the book was rebound. Both the paper and the type are characteristic of the "sixties and seventies" of the last century. These details are given in the hope that they may lead to the discovery of the title of the book [Note from Emperor's Clothes: The introduction, above, states that Publisher had located the text in the British Museum. Today you can buy it from amazon.com].

56

Mr. X believes it must be rare, since, had it not been so, the "Protocols" would have speedily been recognized as a plagiarism by anyone who had read the original.

That the latter is a "fake" could not be maintained for an instant by anyone who had seen it. Its original possessor, the old Okhrana Officer, did not remember where he obtained it, and attached no importance to it. Mr X, glancing at it one day, was struck by a resemblance between a passage which had caught his eye and a phrase in the French edition of the "Protocols" (Edition de la Vieille France, 1920, 5, Rue du Préaux-Cleres, 5, Paris 7th Arrondissement). He followed up the clue, and soon realized that the "Protocols" were to a very large extent as much a paraphrase of the Geneva original as the published version of a War Office or Foreign Office telegram is a paraphrase of the ciphered original. (I)

Before receiving the book from Mr. X, I was, as I have said, incredulous. I did not believe that Sergei Nilus's "Protocols" were authentic; they explained too much by the theory of a vast Jewish conspiracy. Professor Nilus's account of how they were obtained was too melodramatic to be credible, and it was hard to believe that real "Learned Elders of Sion" would not have produced a more intelligent political scheme than the crude and theatrical subtilties of the Protocols. But I could not have believed, had I not seen, that the writer who supplied Nilus with his originals was a careless and shameless plagiarist.

The Geneva book is a very thinly-veiled attack on the despotism of Napoleon III in the form of a series of 25 dialogues divided into four parts. The speakers are Montesquieu and Machiavelli. In the brief preface to his book the anonymous author points out that it contains passages which are applicable to all Governments, "but it particularly personifies a political system which has not varied in its application, for a single day since the fatal and alas! Too distant date when it was enthroned." Its references to the "Haussmannisation" of Paris, to the repressive measures and policy of the French Emperor, to his wasteful financial system, to his foreign wars, to his use of secret societies in foreign policy (cf., his notorious relations with the Carbonari) and his suppression of them in France, to his relations with the Vatican, and to his control of the Press are unmistakable.

MACHIAVELLI-NAPOLEON.

The Geneva Book, or as it will henceforth be called the Geneva Dialogues, opens with the meeting of the spirits of Montesquieu and Machiavelli on a desolate beach in the world of shades. After a lengthy exchange of civilities Montesquieu asks Machiavelli why from an ardent Republican he had become the author of "The Prince" and "the founder of that sombre school of thoughts which has made all crowned heads disciples, but which is well fitted to justify the worst crimes of tyranny." Machiavelli replies that he is a realist and proceeds to justify the teaching of "The Prince," and to explain its applicability to the Western European States of 1864.

In the first six "Geneva Dialogues" Montesquieu is given a chance of argument of which he avails himself. In the seventh dialogue, which corresponds to the fifth, sixth, seventh, and part of the eighth "Protocols," he gives Machiavelli permission to describe at length how he would solve the problem of stabilizing political societies "incessantly disturbed by the spirit of anarchy and revolution." Henceforth Machiavelli or in reality Napoleon III., speaking through Machiavelli, has the lion's share of the dialogue. Montesquieu's contributions thereto become more and more exclamatory; he is profoundly shocked by Machiavelli-Napoleon's defence of an able and ruthless dictatorship, but his counter-arguments grow briefer and weaker. At times, indeed, the author of "L'Espirit des Lois" is made to cut as poor a figure as— parvum componere magno—does Dr. Watson when he attempts to talk criminology to Sherlock Holmes.

DIALOGUE AND "PROTOCOL."

The "Protocols" follow almost the same order as the Dialogues. Dialogues 1-17 generally correspond with "Protocols" 1-19. There are a few exceptions to this. One is in the 18th "Protocol," where, together with paraphrases of passages from the 17th Dialogue ("Geneva Dialogues," pp. 216, 217) there, is an echo of a passage in the 25th "Geneva Dialogue," viz. :–"Quand le malheureux est opprimé il dit 'si le Roi le savait'; Quand on veut se venger, qu on espère un secours, on dit 'le Roi le saura.'" This appears on page 68 of the English edition of the "Protocols" (4th Edition, published by "The Britons," 62, Oxford-street, London, W.) as "In order to exist, the prestige of power must occupy such a position that the people can say among themselves, 'If only the King knew about it,' or 'When the King knows about it.'"

The last five "Protocols" (Nos. 20-24 inclusive) do not contain so many paraphrases of the "Geneva Dialogues" as the first 19. Some of their resemblances and paraphrases are, however, very striking, eg., the following:—

"A loan is an issue of Government paper which entails an obligation to pay interest amounting to a percentage of the total sum of the borrowed money. If a loan is at 5 per cent., then in 20 years the Government would have unnecessarily paid out a sum equal to that of the loan in order to cover the percentage. In 40 years it will have paid twice; and in 60 thrice that amount, but the loan will still remain as an unpaid debt."

— "Protocols," p. 77.

MONTESQUIEU.—"How are loans made? By the issue of bonds entailing on the Government the obligation to pay interest proportionate to the capital it has been paid. Thus, if a loan is at 5 per cent., the State, after 20 years, has paid out a sum equal to the borrowed capital. When 40 years have expired it has paid double, after 60 years triple: yet it remains debtor for the entire capital sum."

—"Geneva Dialogues," p. 250.

But generally speaking "Protocols" 20 and 21, which deal (somewhat unconvincingly) with the financial programme of the Learned Elders, owe less to the "Geneva Dialogues," Nos. 18-21, than to the imagination of the plagiarist author who had for once in a way to show a little originality. This is natural enough since the "Dialogues" in question describe the actual financial policy of the French Imperial Government, while the "Protocols" deal with the future. Again in the last four "Geneva Dialogues" Machiavelli's apotheosis of the Second Empire, being based upon historical facts which took place between 1852 and 1864, obviously furnished scanty material for the plagiarist who wished to prove or, very possibly, had been ordered to prove in the "Protocols" that the ultimate aim of the leaders of Jewry was to give the world a ruler sprung from the House of David.

The scores of parallels between the two books and a theory concerning the methods of the plagiarist and the reasons for the publication of the "Protocols" in 1905 will be the subject of further articles. Meanwhile it is amusing to find that the only subject with which the "Protocols" deal on lines quite contrary to those followed by Machiavelli in the "Dialogues," is the private life of the Sovereign. The last words of the "Protocols" are "Our Sovereign must be irreproachable." The Elders evidently propose to keep the King of Israel in great order. The historical Machiavelli was, we know, rather a scandalous old gentleman, and his shade insists that amorous adventures, so far from injuring a Sovereign's reputation, make him an object of interest and sympathy to "the fairest half of his subjects."

Excerpt form "THE LONDON TIMES",
Wednesday, August 17, 1921, pp. 9, 10

"JEWISH PERIL" EXPOSED.

HISTORIC "FAKE."

DETAILS OF THE FORGERY.

MORE PARALLELS.

We published yesterday an article from our Constantinople Correspondent, which showed that the notorious "Protocols of the Elders of Zion"— one of the mysteries of politics since 1905—were a clumsy forgery, the text being based on a book published in French in 1865.

The book, without title page, was obtained by our Correspondent from a Russian source, and we were able to identify it with a complete copy in the British Museum.

The disclosure, which naturally aroused the greatest interest among those familiar with Jewish questions, finally disposes of the "Protocols" as credible evidence of a Jewish plot against civilization.

We publish below a second article, which gives further close parallels between the language of the Protocols and that attributed to Machiavelli and Montesquieu in the volume dated from Geneva.

PLAGIARISM AT WORK

(From our Constantinople Correspondent.)

While the Geneva Dialogues open with an exchange of compliments between Montesquieu and Machiavelli, which covers seven pages, the author of the Protocols plunges at once in medias res.

One can imagine him hastily turning over those first seven pages of the book which he has been ordered to paraphrase against time, and angrily ejaculating,

60

"Nothing here." But on page 8 of the Dialogues he finds what he wants; the greater part of this page and the next are promptly paraphrased, thus:—

Geneva Dialogues, p. 8.

"Among mankind the evil instinct is mightier than the good. Man is more drawn to evil than to good. Fear and Force have more empire over him than reason....
Every man aims at domination: not one but would be an oppressor if he could: all or almost all are ready to sacrifice the rights of others to their own interests...

"What restrains those beasts of prey which they call men from attacking one another? Brute un-restrained Force in the first stages of social life, then the Law, that is still force regulated by forms. You have consulted all historical sources: everywhere might precedes right. Political Liberty is merely a relative idea...."

-- Protocols, p.I ("The Britons Edition).

"It must be noted that people with corrupt instincts are more numerous than those of noble instinct. Therefore in governing the world the best results are obtained by means of violence and intimidation, and not by academic discussions. Every man aims at power; every one would like to become a dictator if he only could do so, and rare indeed are the men who would not be disposed to sacrifice the welfare of others in order to attain their own personal aims.

"What restrained the wild beasts of prey which we call men? What has ruled them up to now? In the first stages of social life they submitted to brute and blind force, then to law, which in reality is the same force, only masked. From this I am led to deduct that by the law of nature right lies in might. Political freedom is not a fact but an idea."

The gift of liberty according to the Machiavelli of the Geneva Dialogues, of self-government according to the Protocols (page 2), leads speedily to civil and social strife, and the State is soon ruined by internal convulsions or by foreign intervention following on the heels of civil war. Then follows a singular parallel between the two books which deserves quotation:—

Geneva Dialogues. p. 9.

"What arms will they (States) employ in war against foreign enemies? Will the opposing generals communicate their plans of campaign to one another and thus be mutually in a position to defend themselves? Will they mutually ban night attacks, traps, ambushes, battles with inequality of force? Of course not: such combatants would court derision. Are you against the employment of these traps and tricks, of all the strategy indispensable to war against the enemy within, the revolutionary?"

Protocols, p. 2.

"... I would ask the question why is it not immoral for a State which has two enemies, one external and one internal, to use different means of defence against the former to that which it would use against the latter, to make secret plans of defence, to attack him by night or with superior force?"

RIGHT AND WRONG.

Both "Machiavelli" and the author of the Protocols agree (Prot. p. 3, Geneva Dialogues, p. 11) almost in the same words that politics have nothing in common with morality. Right is described in the Protocols as "an abstract idea established by nothing," in the Dialogues as an "infinitely vague" expression. The end, say both, justifies the means. "I pay less attention," says Machiavelli, "to what is good and moral than to what is useful and necessary." The Protocols (p. 4) use the same formula, substituting "profitable" for "useful." According to the protocols he who would rule "must have recourse to cunningness (sic) and hypocrisy." In the second Dialogue (p. 15) Montesquieu reproaches Machiavelli for having "only two words to repeat—'Force' and 'guile.'" Both Machiavelli and the "Elders" of the Protocols preach despotism as the sole safeguard against anarchy. In the Protocols the despotism has to be Jewish and hereditary. Machiavelli's despotism is obviously Napoleonic.

There are scores of other parallels between the books. Fully 50 paragraphs in the Protocols are simply paraphrases of passages in the Dialogues. The quotation per me reges regnant, rightly given in the Vieille France edition of the Protocols (p. 29), while regunt is substituted for regnant in the English version (p. 20), appears on p. 63 of the Geneva Dialogues. Sulla, whom the English version of the Protocols insists on calling "Silla," appears in both books.

"After covering Italy with blood, Sulla reappeared as a simple citizen in Rome: no one durst touch a hair of his head." —Geneva Dialogues, p. 159.

"Remember at the time when Italy was streaming with blood, she did not touch a hair of Silla's head, and he was the man who made her blood pour out." —Protocols, p. 51.

Sulla, who after the proscriptions stalked "in savage grandeur home," is one of the tyrants whom every schoolboy knows and those who believe that Elders of the 33rd Degree are responsible for the Protocols, may say that this is a mere coincidence. But what about the exotic Vishnu, the hundred-armed Hindu deity who appears twice in each book? The following passages never were examples of "unconscious plagiarism."

Geneva Dialogues, p. 141:—

Machiavelli.—"Like the God Vishnu, my press will have a hundred arms, and these arms will give their hands to all the different shades of opinion throughout the country."

Protocols, p. 43:—

"These newspapers, like the Indian god Vishnu, will be possessed of hundreds of hands, each of which will be feeling the pulse of varying public opinion."

Geneva Dialogues, p. 207:—

Montesquieu.—"Now I understand the figure of the god Vishnu; you have a hundred arms like the Indian idol, and each of your fingers touches a spring."

Protocols, p 65:—

[Protocols. —] "Our Government will resemble the Hindu god Vishnu. Each of our hundred hands will hold one spring of the social machinery of State."

TAXATION OF THE PRESS.

The Dialogues and the Protocols alike devote special attention to the Press, and their schemes for muzzling and control thereof are almost identical, absolutely identical, indeed, in many details. Thus Machiavelli on pp. 135 and 136 of the Dialogues expounds the following ingenious scheme:—

Dialogues, pp. 135 and 136 —

"I shall extend the tax on newspapers to books, or rather I shall introduce a stamp duty on books having less than a certain number of pages. A book, for example, with less than 200 or 300 pages will not rank as a book, but as a brochure. I am sure you see the advantage of this scheme. On the one hand I thin (je rarifie) by taxation that cloud of short books which are the more of journalism; on the other hand I force those who wish to escape stamp duty to throw themselves into long and costly compositions, which will hardly ever be sold and scarcely read in such a form."

The Protocols, p. 41, has:—

"We will tax it (the book press) in the same manner as the newspaper Press—that is to say, by means of Excise stamps and deposits. But on books of less than 300 pages we will place a tax twice as heavy. These short books we will classify as pamphlets, which constitute the most virulent form of printed poison. These measures will also compel writers to publish such long works that they will be little read by the public and chiefly so on account of their high price."

Both have the same profound contempt for journalists:

Geneva Dialogues, pp. 145, 146:—

Machiavelli.—"You must know that journalism is a sort of Freemasonry; those who live by it are bound... to one another by the ties of professional discretion; like the augurs of old, they do not lightly divulge the secret of their oracles. They would gain nothing by betraying themselves, for they have mostly won more or less discreditable scars..."

Protocols, p. 44:—

"Already there exists in French journalism a system of Masonic understanding for giving countersigns. All organs of the Press are tied by mutual professional secrets in the manner of the ancient oracles. Not one of its members will betray his knowledge of the secret, if the secret has not been ordered to be made public. No single publisher will have the courage to betray the secret entrusted to him, the reason being that not one of them is admitted into the literary world without bearing the marks of some shady act in his past life."

CONTEMPT FOR THE PEOPLE.

But this contempt is nothing compared to that which both Machiavelli and the Elders evince towards the masses whom tyranny is to reduce to a more than Oriental servitude.

Geneva Dialogues, p. 43:—

Machiavelli.—"You do not know the unbounded meanness of the peoples... groveling before force, pitiless towards the weak, implacable to faults, indulgent to crimes, incapable of supporting the contradictions of a free

64

régime, and patient to the point of martyrdom under the violence of an audacious despotism... giving themselves masters whom they pardon for deeds for the least of which they would have beheaded twenty constitutional kings."

Protocols, p. 15:—

"In their intense meanness the Christian peoples help our independence— when kneeling they crouch before power; when they are pitiless towards the weak; merciless in dealing with faults, and lenient to crimes; when they refuse to recognize the contradictions of freedom; when they are patient to the degree of martyrdom in bearing with the violence of an audacious despotism. At the hands of their present dictators, Premiers, and ministers, they endure abuses for the smallest of which they would have murdered twenty kings."

ATTITUDE TO THE CHURCHES

Both the Elders and Machiavelli propose to make political crime thoroughly unpopular by assimilating the treatment of the political criminal to that of the felon. Both devote not a little attention to police organization and espionage; the creator of Machiavelli had evidently studied Napoleon III.'s police methods, and suffered at the hands of his agents. Each proposes to exercise a severe control over the Bar and the Bench. As regards the Vatican, Machiavelli-Napoleon, with recent Italian history in mind, aims at the complete control of the Papacy. After inflaming popular hatred against the Church of Rome and its clergy, he will intervene to protect the Holy See, as Napoleon III did intervene, when "the chassepots worked wonders." The Learned Elders propose to follow a similar plan: "when the people in their rage thro themselves on to the Vatican we shall appear as its protectors in order to stop bloodshed." Ultimately, of course, they mean to destroy the church. The terrible chiefs of a Pan-Judaic conspiracy could hardly have any other plan of campaign. Machiavelli, naturally, does not go so far. Enough for him if the Pope is safely lodged in the Napoleonic pocket.

Is it necessary to produce further proofs that the majority of the Protocols are simply paraphrases of the Geneva Dialogues, with wicked Hebrew Elders, and finally an Israelite world ruler in the place of Machiavelli-Napoleon III., and the brutish goyim (Gentiles) substituted for the fickle masses, "gripped in a vice by poverty, ridden by sensuality, devoured by ambition," whom Machiavelli intends to win?

The questions now arise, how did the originals become known in Russia, and why were the Protocols invented?

Excerpt form "THE LONDON TIMES",
Thursday, August 18, 1921, pp. 9, 10

THE PROTOCOL FORGERY.

USE IN RUSSIAN POLITICS.

METHODS OF SECRET POLICE.

SOME CONCLUSIONS.

In articles from our Constantinople Correspondent, published yesterday and on Tuesday, we proved that the so-called "Protocols of the Elders of Zion," which have been believed by some since their publication in 1905 to indicate a Jewish plot against civilization, were a clumsy forgery.

To-day our Correspondent reviews the use to which the Protocols were put in recent Russian politics, and summarizes his conclusions.

THE PROTOCOLS IN RUSSIA.

(From Our Constantinople Correspondent.)

There is no evidence as to how the Geneva Dialogues reached Russia. The following theory may be suggested.

The Third Napoleon's secret police, many of whom were Corsicans, must have known the existence of the Dialogues and almost certainly obtained them from some of the many persons arrested on the charge of political conspiracy during the reign of Napoleon III. In the last two decades of the 19th century and in the early years of the 20th there were always a few Corsicans in the Palace Police of the Tsar, and in the Russian secret service. Combining courage with secretiveness, a high average of intelligence with fidelity to his chief, the Corsican makes a first-class secret agent or bodyguard. It is not improbable that Corsicans who had been in the service of Napoleon III., or who had kinsmen in his secret service, brought the Geneva Dialogues to Russia, where some members of the Okhrana or some Court official obtained possession of them. But this is only a theory.

SERGEI NILUS.

As to the Protocols, they were first published in 1905 at Tsarskoye Selo in the second edition of a book entitled "The Great Within the Small," the author of which was Professor Sergei Nilus. Professor Nilus has been described to the writer as a learned, pious, credulous Conservative, who combined much theological and some historical erudition with a singular lack of knowledge of the world. In January, 1917, Nilus, according to the introduction to the French version of the Protocols, published a book, entitled "It is here, at Our Doors!!" in which he republished the Protocols. In this latter work, according to the French version, Professor Nilus states that the manuscript of the Protocols was given him by Nicolaievich Sukhotin, a noble who afterwards became Vice-Governor of Stavropol.

According to the 1905 edition of the Protocols they were obtained by a woman who stole them from "one of the most influential and most highly initiated leaders of Freemasonry. The theft was accomplished at the close of the secret meeting of the 'initiated' in France, that nest of Jewish conspiracy." But in the epilogue to the English version of the Protocols Professor Nilus says, "My friend found them in the safes at the headquarters of the Society of Zion which are at present situated in France." According to the French version of the Protocols, Nilus in his book of 1917 states that the Protocols were notes of a plan submitted to the "Council of Elders" by Theodor Hertzl at the first Zionist Congress which was held at Basle, in August, 1897, and that

Hertzl afterwards complained to the Zionist Committee of Action of the indiscreet publication of confidential information. The Protocols were signed by "Zionist representatives of the 33rd Degree" in Orient Freemasonry and were secretly removed from the complete file of the proceedings of the aforesaid Zionist Congress, which was hidden in the "Chief Zionist office, which is situated in French territory."

Such are Professor Nilus' rather contradictory accounts of the origin of the Protocols. Not a very convincing story! Theodor Hertzl is dead; Sukhotin is dead, and where are the signatures of the Zionist representatives of the 33rd Degree!

Turning to the text of the Protocols, and comparing it with that of the Geneva Dialogues, one is struck by the absence of any effort on the part of the plagiarist to conceal his plagiarisms. The paraphrasing has been very careless; parts of sentences, whole phrases at times, are identical: the development of the thought is the same; there has been no attempt worth mentioning to alter the order of the Geneva Dialogues. The plagiarist has introduced Darwin, Marx, and Nietzsche in one passage in order to be "up to date"; he has given a Jewish colour to "Machiavelli's" schemes for dictatorship, but he has utterly failed to conceal his indebtedness to the Geneva Dialogues. This gives the impression that the real writer of the Protocols, who does not seem to have had anything to do with Nilus and may have been some quite unimportant précis writer employed by the Court or by the Okhrana, was obliged to paraphrase the original at short notice. A proof of Jewish conspiracy was required at once as a weapon for the Conservatives against the Liberal elements in Russia.

Mr. X, the discoverer of the plagiarism, informs me that the Protocols, shortly after their discovery in 1901, four years before their publication by Professor Nilus, served a subsidiary purpose, namely, the first defeat of monsieur Phillippe, a French Hypnotist and thought-reader, who acquired considerable influence over the Tsar and the Tsaritsa at the beginning of the present century. The Court favourite was disliked by certain great personages, and incurred the natural jealousy of the monks, thaumaturgists, and similar adventurers who hoped to capture the Tsar through the Empress in their own interest, or in that of various cliques. Phillippe was not a Jew, but it was easy to represent a Frenchman from "that nest of Jewish conspiracy" as a Zionist agent. Phillippe fell from favour, to return to Russia and find himself once more in the Court's good graces at a later date.

THE FIRST REVOLUTION

But the principal importance of the Protocols was their use during the first Russian Revolution. This revolution was supported by the Jewish element in

Russia, notably by the Jewish Bund. The Okhrana organization knew this perfectly well; it had its Jewish and crypto-Jewish agents, one of whom afterwards assassinated M. Stolypin; it was in league with the powerful Conservative faction; with its allies it sought to gain the Tsar's ear. For many years before the Russian revolution of 1905-1906 there had been a tale of a secret council of Rabbis who plotted ceaselessly against the Orthodox. The publication of the Protocols in 1905 certainly came at an opportune moment for the Conservatives. It is said by some Russians that the manuscript of the Protocols was communicated to the Tsar early in 1905, and that its communication contributed to the fall of the Liberal Prince Sviatopolk-Mirski in that year and the subsequent strong reactionary movement. However that may be, the date and place of publication of Nilus's first edition of the Protocols are most significant now that we know that the originals which were given him were simply paraphrases.

CONCLUSIONS.

The following conclusions are, therefore, forced upon any reader of the two books who has studied Nilus's account of the origin of the Protocols and has some acquaintance with Russian history in the years preceding the revolution of 1905-1906:—

1. The Protocols are largely a paraphrase of the book here provisionally called the "Geneva Dialogues."

2. They were designed to foster the belief among Russian Conservatives, and especially in Court circles, that the prime cause of discontent among the politically minded elements in Russia was not the repressive policy of the bureaucracy, but a world-wide Jewish conspiracy. They thus served as a weapon against the Russian Liberals, who urged the Tsar to make certain concessions to the intelligentsia.

3. The Protocols were paraphrased very hastily and carelessly.

4. Such portions of the Protocols as were not derived from the Geneva Dialogues were probably supplied by the Okhrana, which organization very possibly obtained them from the many Jews it employed to spy on their co-religionists.

So much for the Protocols. They have done harm not so much, in the writer's opinion, by arousing anti-Jewish feeling, which is older than the Protocols and will persist in all countries where there is a Jewish problem until that problem is solved; rather, they have done harm by persuading all sorts of mostly well-to-do people that every recent manifestation of discontent on the part of the poor is an unnatural phenomenon, a factitious agitation caused by a secret society of Jews.

70

THE

PROTOCOLS

OF THE

LEARNED ELDERS

OF ZION

(Translated by Victor E. Marsden)

The author of this translation of the famous Protocols was himself a victim of the Revolution. He had lived for many years in Russia and was married to a Russian lady. Among his other activities in Russia he had been for a number of years a Russian Correspondent of the MORNING POST, a position which he occupied when the Revolution broke out, and his vivid descriptions of events in Russia will still be in the recollection of many of the readers of that Journal. Naturally he was singled out for the anger of the Soviet. On the day that Captain Cromie was murdered by Jews, Victor Marsden was arrested and thrown into the Peter-Paul Prison, expecting every day to have his name called out for execution. This, however, he escaped, and eventually he was allowed to return to England very much of a wreck in bodily health. However, he recovered under treatment and the devoted care of his wife and friends. One of the first things he undertook, as soon as he was able, was this translation of the *Protocols*. Mr. Marsden was eminently well qualified for the work. His intimate acquaintance with Russia, Russian life and the Russian language on the one hand, and his mastery of a terse literary English style on the other, placed him in a position of advantage which few others could claim. The consequence is that we have in his version an eminently readable work, and though the subject-matter is somewhat formless, Mr. Marsden's literary touch reveals the thread running through the twenty-four *Protocols*.

It may be said with truth that this work was carried out at the cost of Mr. Marsden's own life's blood. He told the writer of this *Preface* that he could not stand more than an hour at a time of his work on it in the British Museum, as the diabolical spirit of the matter which he was obliged to turn into English made him positively ill.

Mr. Marsden's connection with the MORNING POST was not severed by his return to England, and he was well enough to accept the post of special correspondent of that journal in the suite of H.R.H., the Prince of Wales on his Empire tour. From this he returned with the Prince, apparently in much better health, but within a few days of his landing he was taken suddenly ill, and died after a very brief illness.

May this work be his crowning monument! In it he has performed an immense service to the English-speaking world, and there can be little doubt that it will take its place in the first rank of the English versions of *"THE PROTOCOLS of the Meetings of the LEARNED ELDERS OF ZION."*

INTRODUCTION

Of the *Protocols* themselves little need be said in the way of introduction. The book in which they are embodied was first published in the year 1897 by Philip Stepanov for private circulation among his intimate friends. The first time Nilus published them was in 1901 in a book called *The Great Within the Small* and reprinted in 1905. A copy of this is in the British Museum bearing the date of its reception, August 10, 1906. All copies that were known to exist in Russia were destroyed in the Kerensky regime, and under his successors the possession of a copy by anyone in Soviet land was a crime sufficient to ensure the owner's of being shot on sight. The fact is in itself sufficient proof of the genuineness of the *Protocols*. The Jewish journals, of course, say that they are a forgery, leaving it to be understood that Professor Nilus, who embodied them in a work of his own, had concocted them for his own purposes.

Mr. Henry Ford, in an interview published in the New York WORLD, February 17th, 1921, put the case for Nilus tersely and convincingly thus:

"The only statement I care to make about the PROTOCOLS is that they fit in with what is going on. They are sixteen years old, and they have fitted the world situation up to this time. THEY FIT IT NOW."

Indeed they do!

The word *"Protocol"* signifies a precis gummed on to the front of a document, a draft of a document, minutes of proceedings. In this instance, *"Protocol"* means minutes of the proceedings of the Meetings of the Learned Elders of Zion. These *Protocols* give the substance of addresses delivered to the innermost circle of the Rulers of Zion. They reveal the converted plan of action of the Jewish Nation developed through the ages and edited by the Elders themselves up to date. Parts and summaries of the plan have been published from time to time during the centuries as the secrets of the Elders have leaked out. The claim of the Jews that the *Protocols* are forgeries is in itself an admission of their genuineness, for they NEVER ATTEMPT TO ANSWER THE FACTS corresponding to the THREATS which the *Protocols* contain, and, indeed, the correspondence between prophecy and fulfillment is too glaring to be set aside or obscured. This the Jews well know and therefore evade.

Captain A.H.M. Ramsay records in his classic, *The Nameless War:* "According to a letter published in *"Plain English"* (a weekly review published by the North British Publishing Co. and edited by the late Lord Alfred Douglas) on 3rd September, 1921:-

"The Learned Elders have been in existence for a much longer period than they have perhaps suspected. My friend, Mr. L. D. van Valckert, of Amsterdam, has recently sent me a letter containing two extracts from the Synagogue at Mulheim. The volume in which they are contained was lost at some period during the Napoleonic Wars, and has recently come into Mr. van Valckert's possession. It is written in German, and contains extracts of letters sent and received by the authorities of the Mulheim Synagogue. The first entry he sends me is of a letter received:-

16th June, 1647.

From O.C. (i.e. Oliver Cromwell), by Ebenezer Pratt.

"In return for financial support will advocate admission of Jews to England: This however impossible while Charles living.

Charles cannot be executed without trial, adequate grounds for which do not at present exist. Therefore advise that Charles be assassinated, but will have nothing to do with arrangements for procuring an assassin, though willing to help in his escape."

In reply was dispatched the following:-

12th July, 1647.

To O.C. by E. Pratt.

"Will grant financial aid as soon as Charles removed and Jews admitted. Assassination too dangerous. Charles shall be given opportunity to escape: His recapture will make trial and execution possible. The support will be liberal, but useless to discuss terms until trial commences."

Captain Ramsay quotes Isaac Disraeli, father of Benjamin, Earl of Beaconsfield, Britain's first Jewish Prime Minister, in his two volume *"Life of Charles I"*, published in 1851: *"The English Revolution under Charles I was unlike any preceding one . . . From that time and event we contemplate in our history the phases of revolution."* There were many more to follow on similar lines, notably in France. In 1897 a further important clue to these mysterious

74

happenings fell into Gentile hands in the shape of the *Protocols of the Elders of Zion.*

In that document we read this remarkable sentence: *"Remember the French Revolution, the secrets of its preparation are well known to us for it was entirely the work of our hands."* (See Protocol No. III, XIV).

In 1865 a certain Jewish Rabbi named Rzeichorn delivered a speech at Prague. It is a very accurate summary of many aspects of the Protocols which would come to light several decades later and was published eleven years later by Sir John Radcliff, who was assassinated shortly afterwards, giving testimony to the powers of the secret organisation of inner elite Jewry even then.

The presumption is strong that the *Protocols* were issued, or reissued, at the First Zionist Congress held at Basle in 1897 under the presidency of the Father of Modern Zionism, the late Theodore Herzl.

There has been recently published a volume of Herzl's "Diaries," a translation of some passages which appeared in the JEWISH CHRONICLE of July 14, 1922. Herzl gives an account of his first visit to England in 1895, and his conversation with Colonel Goldsmid, a Jew brought up as a Christian, an officer in the English Army, and at heart a Jew Nationalist all the time. Goldsmid suggested to Herzl that the best way of expropriating the English aristocracy, and so destroying their power to protect the people of England against Jew domination, was to put excessive taxes on the land. Herzl thought this an excellent idea, and it is now to be found definitely embodied in Protocol VI!

The above extract from Herzl's DIARY is an extremely significant bit of evidence bearing on the existence of the Jew World Plot and authenticity of the *Protocols,* but any reader of intelligence will be able from his own knowledge of recent history and from his own experience to confirm the genuineness of every line of them, and it is in the light of this LIVING comment that all readers are invited to study Mr. Marsden's translation of this terribly inhuman document.

Here is what Dr. Ehrenpreis, Chief Rabbi of Sweden, said in 1924, concerning the *Protocols*: "Long have I been well acquainted with the contents of the *Protocols,* indeed for many years before they were ever published in the Christian press. The Protocols of the Elders of Zion were in point of fact not the original Protocols at all, but a compressed extract of the same. Of the 70

Elders of Zion, in the matter of origin and of the existence of the original *Protocols,* there are only ten men in the entire world who know.

I participated with Dr. Herzl in the first Zionist Congress which was held in Basle in 1897. Herzl was the most prominent figure at the Jewish World Congress. Herzl foresaw, twenty years before we experienced them, the revolution which brought the Great War, and he prepared us for that which was to happen. He foresaw the splitting up of Turkey, that England would obtain control of Palestine. We may expect important developments in the world."

And here is another very significant circumstance. The present successor of Herzl, as leader of the Zionist movement, Dr. Weizmann, quoted one of these sayings at the send-off banquet given to Chief Rabbi Hertz on October 6, 1920. The Chief Rabbi was on the point of leaving for HIS Empire tour of H.R.H., the Prince of Wales. And this is the "saying" of the Sages which Dr. Weizmann quoted: *"A beneficent protection which God has instituted in the life of the Jew is that He has dispersed him all over the world."* (JEWISH GUARDIAN, Oct. 8, 1920.)

Now compare this with the last clause of but one of Protocol XI.

"God has granted to us, His Chosen People, the gift of dispersion, and from this, which appears to all eyes to be our weakness, has come forth all our strength, which has now brought us to the threshold of sovereignty over all the world."

The remarkable correspondence between these passages proves several things. It proves that the Learned Elders exist. It proves that Dr. Weizmann knows all about them. It proves that the desire for a *"National Home"* in Palestine is only camouflage and an infinitesimal part of the Jew's real object. It proves that the Jews of the world have no intention of settling in Palestine or any separate country, and that their annual prayer that they may all meet *"Next Year in Jerusalem"* is merely a piece of their characteristic make-believe. It also demonstrates that the Jews are now a world menace, and that the Aryan races will have to domicile them permanently out of Europe..

WHO ARE THE ELDERS?

This is a secret which has not been revealed. They are the Hidden Hand. They are not the *"Board of Deputies"* (the Jewish Parliament in England) or the *"Universal Israelite Alliance"* which sits in Paris. But the late Walter Rathenau of the Allgemeiner Electricitaets Gesellschaft has thrown a little light on the subject and doubtless he was in possession of their names, being, in all likelihood, one of the chief leaders himself. Writing in the WIENER FREIE PRESSE, December 24, 1912, he said:

"Three hundred men, each of whom knows all the others, govern the fate of the European continent, and they elect their successors from their entourage."

In the year 1844, on the eve of the Jewish Revolution of 1848, Benjamin Disraeli, whose real name was Israel, and who was a *"damped,"* or baptized Jew, published his novel, CONINGSBY, in which occurs this ominous passage:

"The world is governed by very different personages from what is imagined by those who are not behind the scenes."

And he went on to show that these personages were all Jews.

Now that Providence has brought to the light of day these secret *Protocols* all men may clearly see the hidden personages specified by Disraeli at work "behind the scenes" of all the Governments. This revelation entails on all peoples the grave responsibility of examining and revising AU FOND their attitude towards the Race and Nation which boasts of its survival over all Empires.

Notes I. - "Agentur" and "The Political."

There are two words in this translation which are unusual, the word "AGENTUR" and "political" used as a substantive, AGENTUR appears to be a word adopted from the original and it means the whole body of agents and agencies made use of by the Elders, whether members of the tribe or their Gentile tools.

By *"the Political"* Mr. Marsden means, not exactly the *"body politic"* but the entire machinery of politics.

Notes II - The Symbolic Snake of Judaism.

Protocol III opens with a reference to the Symbolic Snake of Judaism. In his Epilogue to the 1905 Edition of the Protocols, Nilus gives the following interesting account of this symbol:

"According to the records of secret Jewish Zionism, Solomon and other Jewish learned men already, in 929 B.C., thought out a scheme in theory for a peaceful conquest of the whole universe by Zion. As history developed, this scheme was worked out in detail and completed by men who were subsequently initiated in this question. These learned men decided by peaceful means to conquer the world for Zion with the slyness of the Symbolic Snake, whose head was to represent those who have been initiated into the plans of the Jewish administration, and the body of the Snake to represent the Jewish people - the administration was always kept secret, EVEN FROM THE JEWISH NATION ITSELF. As this Snake penetrated into the hearts of the nations which it encountered it undermined and devoured all the non-Jewish power of these States. It is foretold that the Snake has still to finish its work, strictly adhering to the designed plan, until the course which it has to run is closed by the return of its head to Zion and until, by this means, the Snake has completed its round of Europe and has encircled it - and until, by dint of enchaining Europe, it has encompassed the whole world. This it is to accomplish by using every endeavor to subdue the other countries by an ECONOMICAL CONQUEST. The return of the head of the Snake to Zion can only be accomplished after the power of all the Sovereign of Europe has been laid low, that is to say, when by means of economic crises and wholesale destruction effected everywhere, there shall have been brought about a spiritual demoralization and a moral corruption, chiefly with the assistance of Jewish women masquerading as French, Italians, etc.. These are the surest spreaders of licentiousness into the lives of the leading men at the heads of nations. A map of the course of the Symbolic Snake is shown as follows: - Its first stage in Europe was in 429 B.C. in Greece, where, about the time of Pericles, the Snake first started eating into the power of that country. The second stage was in Rome in the time of Augustus, about 69 B.C.. The third in Madrid in the time of Charles V, in A.D. 1552. The fourth in Paris about 1790, in the time of Louis XVI. The fifth in London from 1814 onwards (after the downfall of Napoleon). The sixth in Berlin in 1871 after the Franco-Prussian war. The seventh in St. Petersburg, over which is drawn the head of the Snake under the date of 1881. [This "Snake" is now being drawn through the Americas and in the United States of America, it has been partially identified as the "Council on Foreign Relations" (C.F.R.) and the "Trilateral Commission"]. All these States which the Snake traversed have had the foundations of their constitutions shaken, Germany, with its apparent power, forming no exception to the rule. In economic conditions, England and Germany are spared, but only till the conquest of Russia is accomplished by the Snake, on which at present [i.e., 1905] all its efforts are concentrated. The further course of the Snake is not shown on this map, but arrows indicate its next movement towards Moscow, Kieft and Odessa. It is now well known to us to what extent the latter cities form the centres of the militant Jewish race. Constantinople is shown as the last stage of the Snake's course before it reaches Jerusalem. (This map was drawn years before the occurrence of the "Young Turk" - i.e., Jewish - Revolution in Turkey).

78

{Note: The term *"Goyim,"* meaning *Gentile* or *non-Jews,* is used throughout the *Protocols* and is retained by Mr. Marsden.}

PROTOCOL No. I

1. ....Putting aside fine phrases we shall speak of the significance of each thought: by comparisons and deductions we shall throw light upon surrounding facts.

2. What I am about to set forth, then, is our system from the two points of view, that of ourselves and that of the GOYIM [i.e., non-Jews].

3. It must be noted that men with bad instincts are more in number than the good, and therefore the best results in governing them are attained by violence and terrorisation, and not by academic discussions. Every man aims at power, everyone would like to become a dictator if only he could, and rare indeed are the men who would not be willing to sacrifice the welfare of all for the sake of securing their own welfare.

4. What has restrained the beasts of prey who are called men? What has served for their guidance hitherto?

5. In the beginnings of the structure of society, they were subjected to brutal and blind force; afterwards - to Law, which is the same force, only disguised. I draw the conclusion that by the law of nature, right lies in force.

6. Political freedom is an idea but not a fact. This idea one must know how to apply whenever it appears necessary with this bait of an idea to attract the masses of the people to one's party for the purpose of crushing another who is in authority. This task is rendered easier if the opponent has himself been infected with the idea of freedom, SO-CALLED LIBERALISM, and, for the sake of an idea, is willing to yield some of his power. It is precisely here that the triumph of our theory appears; the slackened reins of government are immediately, by the law of life, caught up and gathered together by a new hand, because the blind might of the nation cannot for one single day exist without guidance, and the new authority merely fits into the place of the old already weakened by liberalism.

7. In our day the power which has replaced that of the rulers who were liberal is the power of Gold. Time was when Faith ruled. The idea of freedom is impossible of realization because no one knows how to use it with moderation. It is enough to hand over a people to self-government for a certain length of time for that people to be turned into a disorganized mob. From that moment on we get internecine strife which soon develops into battles between classes, in the midst of which States burn down and their importance is reduced to that of a heap of ashes.

8. Whether a State exhausts itself in its own convulsions, whether its internal discord brings it under the power of external foes - in any case it can be accounted irretrievably lost: IT IS IN OUR POWER. The despotism of Capital, which is entirely in our hands, reaches out to it a straw that the State, willy-nilly, must take hold of: if not - it goes to the bottom.

9. Should anyone of a liberal mind say that such reflections as the above are immoral, I would put the following questions: If every State has two foes and if in regard to the external foe it is allowed and not considered immoral to use every manner and art of conflict, as for example to keep the enemy in ignorance of plans of attack and defense, to attack him by night or in superior numbers, then in what way can the same means in regard to a worse foe, the destroyer of the structure of society and the commonweal, be called immoral and not permissible?

10. Is it possible for any sound logical mind to hope with any success to guide crowds by the aid of reasonable counsels and arguments, when any objection or contradiction, senseless though it may be, can be made and when such objection may find more favor with the people, whose powers of reasoning are superficial? Men in masses and the men of the masses, being guided solely by petty passions, paltry beliefs, traditions and sentimental theorems, fall a prey to party dissension, which hinders any kind of agreement even on the basis of a perfectly reasonable argument. Every resolution of a crowd depends upon a chance or packed majority, which, in its ignorance of political secrets, puts forth some ridiculous resolution that lays in the administration a seed of anarchy.

11. The political has nothing in common with the moral. The ruler who is governed by the moral is not a skilled politician, and is therefore unstable on his throne. He who wishes to rule must have recourse both to cunning and to make-believe. Great national qualities, like frankness and honesty, are vices in politics, for they bring down rulers from their thrones more effectively and

80

more certainly than the most powerful enemy. Such qualities must be the attributes of the kingdoms of the GOYIM, but we must in no wise be guided by them.

RIGHT IS MIGHT

12. Our right lies in force. The word *"right"* is an abstract thought and proved by nothing. The word means no more than: *Give me what I want in order that thereby I may have a proof that I am stronger than you.*

13. Where does right begin? Where does it end?

14. In any State in which there is a bad organization of authority, an impersonality of laws and of the rulers who have lost their personality amid the flood of rights ever multiplying out of liberalism, I find a new right - to attack by the right of the strong, and to scatter to the winds all existing forces of order and regulation, to reconstruct all institutions and to become the sovereign lord of those who have left to us the rights of their power by laying them down voluntarily in their liberalism.

15. Our power in the present tottering condition of all forms of power will be more invincible than any other, because it will remain invisible until the moment when it has gained such strength that no cunning can any longer undermine it.

16. Out of the temporary evil we are now compelled to commit will emerge the good of an unshakable rule, which will restore the regular course of the machinery of the national life, brought to naught by liberalism. The result justifies the means. Let us, however, in our plans, direct our attention not so much to what is good and moral as to what is necessary and useful.

17. Before us is a plan in which is laid down strategically the line from which we cannot deviate without running the risk of seeing the labor of many centuries brought to naught.

18. In order to elaborate satisfactory forms of action it is necessary to have regard to the rascality, the slackness, the instability of the mob, its lack of capacity to understand and respect the conditions of its own life, or its own welfare. It must be understood that the might of a mob is blind, senseless and un-reasoning force ever at the mercy of a suggestion from any side. The blind cannot lead the blind without bringing them into the abyss; consequently, members of the mob, upstarts from the people even though they should be as a

genius for wisdom, yet having no understanding of the political, cannot come forward as leaders of the mob without bringing the whole nation to ruin.

19. Only one trained from childhood for independent rule can have understanding of the words that can be made up of the political alphabet.

20. A people left to itself, i.e., to upstarts from its midst, brings itself to ruin by party dissensions excited by the pursuit of power and honors and the disorders arising therefrom. Is it possible for the masses of the people calmly and without petty jealousies to form judgment, to deal with the affairs of the country, which cannot be mixed up with personal interest? Can they defend themselves from an external foe? It is unthinkable; for a plan broken up into as many parts as there are heads in the mob, loses all homogeneity, and thereby becomes unintelligible and impossible of execution.

WE ARE DESPOTS

21. It is only with a despotic ruler that plans can be elaborated extensively and clearly in such a way as to distribute the whole properly among the several parts of the machinery of the State: from this the conclusion is inevitable that a satisfactory form of government for any country is one that concentrates in the hands of one responsible person. Without an absolute despotism there can be no existence for civilization which is carried on not by the masses but by their guide, whosoever that person may be. The mob is savage, and displays its savagery at every opportunity. The moment the mob seizes freedom in its hands it quickly turns to anarchy, which in itself is the highest degree of savagery.

22. Behold the alcoholic animals, bemused with drink, the right to an immoderate use of which comes along with freedom. It is not for us and ours to walk that road. The peoples of the GOYIM are bemused with alcoholic liquors; their youth has grown stupid on classicism and from early immorality, into which it has been inducted by our special agents - by tutors, lackeys, governesses in the houses of the wealthy, by clerks and others, by our women in the places of dissipation frequented by the GOYIM. In the number of these last I count also the so-called *"society ladies,"* voluntary followers of the others in corruption and luxury.

23. Our countersign is - Force and Make-believe. Only force conquers in political affairs, especially if it be concealed in the talents essential to statesmen. Violence must be the principle, and cunning and make-believe the rule for governments which do not want to lay down their crowns at the feet of

agents of some new power. This evil is the one and only means to attain the end, the good. Therefore we must not stop at bribery, deceit and treachery when they should serve towards the attainment of our end. In politics one must know how to seize the property of others without hesitation if by it we secure submission and sovereignty.

24. Our State, marching along the path of peaceful conquest, has the right to replace the horrors of war by less noticeable and more satisfactory sentences of death, necessary to maintain the terror which tends to produce blind submission. Just but merciless severity is the greatest factor of strength in the State: not only for the sake of gain but also in the name of duty, for the sake of victory, we must keep to the programme of violence and make-believe. The doctrine of squaring accounts is precisely as strong as the means of which it makes use. Therefore it is not so much by the means themselves as by the doctrine of severity that we shall triumph and bring all governments into subjection to our super-government. It is enough for them to know that we are too merciless for all disobedience to cease.

WE SHALL END LIBERTY

25. Far back in ancient times we were the first to cry among the masses of the people the words *"Liberty, Equality, Fraternity,"* words many times repeated since these days by stupid poll-parrots who, from all sides around, flew down upon these baits and with them carried away the well-being of the world, true freedom of the individual, formerly so well guarded against the pressure of the mob. The would-be wise men of the GOYIM, the intellectuals, could not make anything out of the uttered words in their abstractedness; did not see that in nature there is no equality, cannot be freedom: that Nature herself has established inequality of minds, of characters, and capacities, just as immutably as she has established subordination to her laws: never stopped to think that the mob is a blind thing, that upstarts elected from among it to bear rule are, in regard to the political, the same blind men as the mob itself, that the adept, though he be a fool, can yet rule, whereas the non-adept, even if he were a genius, understands nothing in the political - to all those things the GOYIM paid no regard; yet all the time it was based upon these things that dynastic rule rested: the father passed on to the son a knowledge of the course of political affairs in such wise that none should know it but members of the dynasty and none could betray it to the governed. As time went on, the meaning of the dynastic transference of the true position of affairs in the political was lost, and this aided the success of our cause.

26. In all corners of the earth the words *"Liberty, Equality, Fraternity,"* brought to our ranks, thanks to our blind agents, whole legions who bore our

banners with enthusiasm. And all the time these words were canker-worms at work boring into the well-being of the GOYIM, putting an end everywhere to peace, quiet, solidarity and destroying all the foundations of the GOY States. As you will see later, this helped us to our triumph: it gave us the possibility, among other things, of getting into our hands the master card - the destruction of the privileges, or in other words of the very existence of the aristocracy of the GOYIM, that class which was the only defense peoples and countries had against us. On the ruins of the eternal and genealogical aristocracy of the GOYIM we have set up the aristocracy of our educated class headed by the aristocracy of money. The qualifications for this aristocracy we have established in wealth, which is dependent upon us, and in knowledge, for which our learned elders provide the motive force.

27. Our triumph has been rendered easier by the fact that in our relations with the men, whom we wanted, we have always worked upon the most sensitive chords of the human mind, upon the cash account, upon the cupidity, upon the insatiability for material needs of man; and each one of these human weaknesses, taken alone, is sufficient to paralyze initiative, for it hands over the will of men to the disposition of him who has bought their activities.

28. The abstraction of freedom has enabled us to persuade the mob in all countries that their government is nothing but the steward of the people who are the owners of the country, and that the steward may be replaced like a worn-out glove.

29. It is this possibility of replacing the representatives of the people which has placed at our disposal, and, as it were, given us the power of appointment.

PROTOCOL No. 2

I. It is indispensable for our purpose that wars, so far as possible, should not result in territorial gains: war will thus be brought on to the economic ground, where the nations will not fail to perceive in the assistance we give the strength of our predominance, and this state of things will put both sides at the mercy of our international AGENTUR; which possesses millions of eyes ever on the watch and unhampered by any limitations whatsoever. Our international rights will then wipe out national rights, in the proper sense of right, and will rule the nations precisely as the civil law of States rules the relations of their subjects among themselves.

2. The administrators, whom we shall choose from among the public, with strict regard to their capacities for servile obedience, will not be persons trained

in the arts of government, and will therefore easily become pawns in our game in the hands of men of learning and genius who will be their advisers, specialists bred and reared from early childhood to rule the affairs of the whole world. As is well known to you, these specialists of ours have been drawing to fit them for rule the information they need from our political plans from the lessons of history, from observations made of the events of every moment as it passes. The GOYIM are not guided by practical use of unprejudiced historical observation, but by theoretical routine without any critical regard for consequent results. We need not, therefore, take any account of them - let them amuse themselves until the hour strikes, or live on hopes of new forms of enterprising pastime, or on the memories of all they have enjoyed. For them let that play the principal part which we have persuaded them to accept as the dictates of science (theory). It is with this object in view that we are constantly, by means of our press, arousing a blind confidence in these theories. The intellectuals of the GOYIM will puff themselves up with their knowledges and without any logical verification of them will put into effect all the information available from science, which our AGENTUR specialists have cunningly pieced together for the purpose of educating their minds in the direction we want.

DESTRUCTIVE EDUCATION

3. Do not suppose for a moment that these statements are empty words: think carefully of the successes we arranged for Darwinism, Marxism, Nietzsche-ism. To us Jews, at any rate, it should be plain to see what a disintegrating importance these directives have had upon the minds of the GOYIM.

4. It is indispensable for us to take account of the thoughts, characters, tendencies of the nations in order to avoid making slips in the political and in the direction of administrative affairs. The triumph of our system of which the component parts of the machinery may be variously disposed according to the temperament of the peoples met on our way, will fail of success if the practical application of it be not based upon a summing up of the lessons of the past in the light of the present.

5. In the hands of the States of to-day there is a great force that creates the movement of thought in the people, and that is the Press. The part played by the Press is to keep pointing our requirements supposed to be indispensable, to give voice to the complaints of the people, to express and to create discontent. It is in the Press that the triumph of freedom of speech finds its incarnation. But the GOYIM States have not known how to make use of this force; and it has fallen into our hands. Through the Press we have gained the power to influence while remaining ourselves in the shade; thanks to the Press we have

got the GOLD in our hands, notwithstanding that we have had to gather it out of the oceans of blood and tears. But it has paid us, though we have sacrificed many of our people. Each victim on our side is worth in the sight of God a thousand GOYIM.

PROTOCOL No. 3

1. To-day I may tell you that our goal is now only a few steps off. There remains a small space to cross and the whole long path we have trodden is ready now to close its cycle of the Symbolic Snake, by which we symbolize our people. When this ring closes, all the States of Europe will be locked in its coil as in a powerful vice.

2. The constitution scales of these days will shortly break down, for we have established them with a certain lack of accurate balance in order that they may oscillate incessantly until they wear through the pivot on which they turn. The GOYIM are under the impression that they have welded them sufficiently strong and they have all along kept on expecting that the scales would come into equilibrium. But the pivots - the kings on their thrones - are hemmed in by their representatives, who play the fool, distraught with their own uncontrolled and irresponsible power. This power they owe to the terror which has been breathed into the palaces. As they have no means of getting at their people, into their very midst, the kings on their thrones are no longer able to come to terms with them and so strengthen themselves against seekers after power. We have made a gulf between the far-seeing Sovereign Power and the blind force of the people so that both have lost all meaning, for like the blind man and his stick, both are powerless apart.

3. In order to incite seekers after power to a misuse of power we have set all forces in opposition one to another, breaking up their liberal tendencies towards independence. To this end we have stirred up every form of enterprise, we have armed all parties, we have set up authority as a target for every ambition. Of States we have made gladiatorial arenas where a lot of confused issues contend ... A little more, and disorders and bankruptcy will be universal ...

4. Babblers, inexhaustible, have turned into oratorical contests the sittings of Parliament and Administrative Boards. Bold journalists and unscrupulous pamphleteers daily fall upon executive officials. Abuses of power will put the final touch in preparing all institutions for their overthrow and everything will fly skyward under the blows of the maddened mob.

POVERTY OUR WEAPON

5. All people are chained down to heavy toil by poverty more firmly than ever. They were chained by slavery and serfdom; from these, one way and another, they might free themselves. These could be settled with, but from want they will never get away. We have included in the constitution such rights as to the masses appear fictitious and not actual rights. All these so-called *"Peoples Rights"* can exist only in idea, an idea which can never be realized in practical life. What is it to the proletariat laborer, bowed double over his heavy toil, crushed by his lot in life, if talkers get the right to babble, if journalists get the right to scribble any nonsense side by side with good stuff, once the proletariat has no other profit out of the constitution save only those pitiful crumbs which we fling them from our table in return for their voting in favor of what we dictate, in favor of the men we place in power, the servants of our AGENTUR ... Republican rights for a poor man are no more than a bitter piece of irony, for the necessity he is under of toiling almost all day gives him no present use of them, but the other hand robs him of all guarantee of regular and certain earnings by making him dependent on strikes by his comrades or lockouts by his masters.

WE SUPPORT COMMUNISM

6. The people, under our guidance, have annihilated the aristocracy, who were their one and only defense and foster-mother for the sake of their own advantage which is inseparably bound up with the well-being of the people. Nowadays, with the destruction of the aristocracy, the people have fallen into the grips of merciless money-grinding scoundrels who have laid a pitiless and cruel yoke upon the necks of the workers.

7. We appear on the scene as alleged saviours of the worker from this oppression when we propose to him to enter the ranks of our fighting forces - Socialists, Anarchists, Communists - to whom we always give support in accordance with an alleged brotherly rule (of the solidarity of all humanity) of our SOCIAL MASONRY. The aristocracy, which enjoyed by law the labor of the workers, was interested in seeing that the workers were well fed, healthy, and strong. We are interested in just the opposite - in the diminution. the KILLING OUT OF THE GOYIM. Our power is in the chronic shortness of food and physical weakness of the worker because by all that this implies he is made the slave of our will, and he will not find in his own authorities either strength or energy to set against our will. Hunger creates the right of capital to rule the worker more surely than it was given to the aristocracy by the legal authority of kings.

8. By want and the envy and hatred which it engenders we shall move the mobs and with their hands we shall wipe out all those who hinder us on our way.

9. WHEN THE HOUR STRIKES FOR OUR SOVEREIGN LORD OF ALL THE WORLD TO BE CROWNED IT IS THESE SAME HANDS WHICH WILL SWEEP AWAY EVERYTHING THAT MIGHT BE A HINDRANCE THERETO. (The Biblical *"Anti-Christ?"*)

10. The GOYIM have lost the habit of thinking unless prompted by the suggestions of our specialists. Therefore they do not see the urgent necessity of what we, when our kingdom comes, shall adopt at once, namely this, that IT IS ESSENTIAL TO TEACH IN NATIONAL SCHOOLS ONE SIMPLE, TRUE PIECE OF KNOWLEDGE, THE BASIS OF ALL KNOWLEDGE - THE KNOWLEDGE OF THE STRUCTURE OF HUMAN LIFE, OF SOCIAL EXISTENCE, WHICH REQUIRES DIVISION OF LABOR, AND, CONSEQUENTLY, THE DIVISION OF MEN INTO CLASSES AND CONDITIONS. It is essential for all to know that OWING TO DIFFERENCE IN THE OBJECTS OF HUMAN ACTIVITY THERE CANNOT BE ANY EQUALITY, that he, who by any act of his compromises a whole class, cannot be equally responsible before the law with him who affects no one but only his own honor. The true knowledge of the structure of society, into the secrets of which we do not admit the GOYIM, would demonstrate to all men that the positions and work must be kept within a certain circle, that they may not become a source of human suffering, arising from an education which does not correspond with the work which individuals are called upon to do. After a thorough study of this knowledge, the peoples will voluntarily submit to authority and accept such position as is appointed them in the State. In the present state of knowledge and the direction we have given to its development of the people, blindly believing things in print - cherishes - thanks to promptings intended to mislead and to its own ignorance - a blind hatred towards all conditions which it considers above itself, for it has no understanding of the meaning of class and condition.

JEWS WILL BE SAFE

11. THIS HATRED WILL BE STILL FURTHER MAGNIFIED BY THE EFFECTS of an ECONOMIC CRISES, which will stop dealing on the exchanges and bring industry to a standstill. We shall create by all the secret subterranean methods open to us and with the aid of gold, which is all in our hands, A UNIVERSAL ECONOMIC CRISES WHEREBY WE SHALL THROW UPON THE STREETS WHOLE MOBS OF WORKERS SIMULTANEOUSLY IN ALL THE COUNTRIES OF EUROPE. These mobs will rush delightedly to shed the blood of those whom, in the simplicity

of their ignorance, they have envied from their cradles, and whose property they will then be able to loot.

12. "OURS" THEY WILL NOT TOUCH, BECAUSE THE MOMENT OF ATTACK WILL BE KNOWN TO US AND WE SHALL TAKE MEASURES TO PROTECT OUR OWN.

13. We have demonstrated that progress will bring all the GOYIM to the sovereignty of reason. Our despotism will be precisely that; for it will know how, by wise severities, to pacificate all unrest, to cauterize liberalism out of all institutions.

14. When the populace has seen that all sorts of concessions and indulgences are yielded it, in the same name of freedom it has imagined itself to be sovereign lord and has stormed its way to power, but, naturally like every other blind man, it has come upon a host of stumbling blocks. IT HAS RUSHED TO FIND A GUIDE, IT HAS NEVER HAD THE SENSE TO RETURN TO THE FORMER STATE and it has laid down its plenipotentiary powers at OUR feet. Remember the French Revolution, to which it was we who gave the name of *"Great"*: the secrets of its preparations are well known to us for it was wholly the work of our hands.

15. Ever since that time we have been leading the peoples from one disenchantment to another, so that in the end they should turn also from us in favor of that KING-DESPOT OF THE BLOOD OF ZION, WHOM WE ARE PREPARING FOR THE WORLD.

16. At the present day we are, as an international force, invincible, because if attacked by some we are supported by other States. It is the bottomless rascality of the GOYIM peoples, who crawl on their bellies to force, but are merciless towards weakness, unsparing to faults and indulgent to crimes, unwilling to bear the contradictions of a free social system but patient unto martyrdom under the violence of a bold despotism - it is those qualities which are aiding us to independence. From the premier-dictators of the present day, the GOYIM peoples suffer patiently and bear such abuses as for the least of them they would have beheaded twenty kings.

17. What is the explanation of this phenomenon, this curious inconsequence of the masses of the peoples in their attitude towards what would appear to be events of the same order?

18. It is explained by the fact that these dictators whisper to the peoples through their agents that through these abuses they are inflicting injury on the States with the highest purpose - to secure the welfare of the peoples, the international brotherhood of them all, their solidarity and equality of rights. Naturally they do not tell the peoples that this unification must be accomplished only under our sovereign rule.

19. And thus the people condemn the upright and acquit the guilty, persuaded ever more and more that it can do whatsoever it wishes. Thanks to this state of things, the people are destroying every kind of stability and creating disorders at every step.

20. The word *"freedom"* brings out the communities of men to fight against every kind of force, against every kind of authority even against God and the laws of nature. For this reason we, when we come into our kingdom, shall have to erase this word from the lexicon of life as implying a principle of brute force which turns mobs into bloodthirsty beasts.

21. These beasts, it is true, fall asleep again every time when they have drunk their fill of blood, and at such time can easily be riveted into their chains. But if they be not given blood they will not sleep and continue to struggle.

PROTOCOL No. 4

1. Every republic passes through several stages. The first of these is comprised in the early days of mad raging by the blind mob, tossed hither and thither, right and left: the second is demagogy from which is born anarchy, and that leads inevitably to despotism - not any longer legal and overt, and therefore responsible despotism, but to unseen and secretly hidden, yet nevertheless sensibly felt despotism in the hands of some secret organization or other, whose acts are the more unscrupulous inasmuch as it works behind a screen, behind the backs of all sorts of agents, the changing of whom not only does not injuriously affect but actually aids the secret force by saving it, thanks to continual changes, from the necessity of expanding its resources on the rewarding of long services.

2. Who and what is in a position to overthrow an invisible force? And this is precisely what our force is. GENTILE masonry blindly serves as a screen for us and our objects, but the plan of action of our force, even its very abiding-place, remains for the whole people an unknown mystery.

WE SHALL DESTROY GOD

3. But even freedom might be harmless and have its place in the State economy without injury to the well-being of the peoples if it rested upon the foundation of faith in God, upon the brotherhood of humanity, unconnected with the conception of equality, which is negatived by the very laws of creation, for they have established subordination. With such a faith as this a people might be governed by a wardship of parishes, and would walk contentedly and humbly under the guiding hand of its spiritual pastor submitting to the dispositions of God upon earth. This is the reason why IT IS INDISPENSABLE FOR US TO UNDERMINE ALL FAITH, TO TEAR OUT OF THE MIND OF THE *"GOYIM"* THE VERY PRINCIPLE OF GOD-HEAD AND THE SPIRIT, AND TO PUT IN ITS PLACE ARITHMETICAL CALCULATIONS AND MATERIAL NEEDS.

4. In order to give the GOYIM no time to think and take note, their minds must be diverted towards industry and trade. Thus, all the nations will be swallowed up in the pursuit of gain and in the race for it will not take note of their common foe. But again, in order that freedom may once for all disintegrate and ruin the communities of the GOYIM, we must put industry on a speculative basis: the result of this will be that what is withdrawn from the land by industry will slip through the hands and pass into speculation, that is, to our classes.

5. The intensified struggle for superiority and shocks delivered to economic life will create, nay, have already created, disenchanted, cold and heartless communities. Such communities will foster a strong aversion towards the higher political and towards religion. Their only guide is gain, that is Gold, which they will erect into a veritable cult, for the sake of those material delights which it can give. Then will the hour strike when, not for the sake of attaining the good, not even to win wealth, but solely out of hatred towards the privileged, the lower classes of the GOYIM will follow our lead against our rivals for power, the intellectuals of the GOYIM.

PROTOCOL No. 5

1. What form of administrative rule can be given to communities in which corruption has penetrated everywhere, communities where riches are attained only by the clever surprise tactics of semi-swindling tricks; where loseness reigns: where morality is maintained by penal measures and harsh laws but not by voluntarily accepted principles: where the feelings towards faith and country are obligated by cosmopolitan convictions? What form of rule is to be given to these communities if not that despotism which I shall describe to you later?

We shall create an intensified centralization of government in order to grip in our hands all the forces of the community. We shall regulate mechanically all the actions of the political life of our subjects by new laws. These laws will withdraw one by one all the indulgences and liberties which have been permitted by the GOYIM, and our kingdom will be distinguished by a despotism of such magnificent proportions as to be at any moment and in every place in a position to wipe out any GOYIM who oppose us by deed or word.

2. We shall be told that such a despotism as I speak of is not consistent with the progress of these days, but I will prove to you that it is.

3. In the times when the peoples looked upon kings on their thrones as on a pure manifestation of the will of God, they submitted without a murmur to the despotic power of kings: but from the day when we insinuated into their minds the conception of their own rights they began to regard the occupants of thrones as mere ordinary mortals. The holy unction of the Lord's Anointed has fallen from the heads of kings in the eyes of the people, and when we also robbed them of their faith in God the might of power was flung upon the streets into the place of public proprietorship and was seized by us.

MASSES LED BY LIES

4. Moreover, the art of directing masses and individuals by means of cleverly manipulated theory and verbiage, by regulations of life in common and all sorts of other quirks, in all which the GOYIM understand nothing, belongs likewise to the specialists of our administrative brain. Reared on analysis, observation, on delicacies of fine calculation, in this species of skill we have no rivals, any more than we have either in the drawing up of plans of political actions and solidarity. In this respect the Jesuits alone might have compared with us, but we have contrived to discredit them in the eyes of the unthinking mob as an overt organization, while we ourselves all the while have kept our secret organization in the shade. However, it is probably all the same to the world who is its sovereign lord, whether the head of Catholicism or our despot of the blood of Zion! But to us, the Chosen People, it is very far from being a matter of indifference.

5. FOR A TIME PERHAPS WE MIGHT BE SUCCESSFULLY DEALT WITH BY A COALITION OF THE "GOYIM" OF ALL THE WORLD: but from this danger we are secured by the discord existing among them whose roots are so deeply seated that they can never now be plucked up. We have set one against another the personal and national reckonings of the GOYIM, religious and race hatreds, which we have fostered into a huge growth in the

92

course of the past twenty centuries. This is the reason why there is not one State which would anywhere receive support if it were to raise its arm, for every one of them must bear in mind that any agreement against us would be unprofitable to itself. We are too strong - there is no evading our power. THE NATIONS CANNOT COME TO EVEN AN INCONSIDERABLE PRIVATE AGREEMENT WITHOUT OUR SECRETLY HAVING A HAND IN IT.

6. PER ME REGES REGNANT. *"It is through me that Kings reign."* And it was said by the prophets that we were chosen by God Himself to rule over the whole earth. God has endowed us with genius that we may be equal to our task. Were genius in the opposite camp it would still struggle against us, but even so, a newcomer is no match for the old-established settler: the struggle would be merciless between us, such a fight as the world has never seen. Aye, and the genius on their side would have arrived too late. All the wheels of the machinery of all States go by the force of the engine, which is in our hands, and that engine of the machinery of States is - Gold. The science of political economy invented by our learned elders has for long past been giving royal prestige to capital.

MONOPOLY CAPITAL

7. Capital, if it is to co-operate untrammeled, must be free to establish a monopoly of industry and trade: this is already being put in execution by an unseen hand in all quarters of the world. This freedom will give political force to those engaged in industry, and that will help to oppress the people. Nowadays it is more important to disarm the peoples than to lead them into war: more important to use for our advantage the passions which have burst into flames than to quench their fire: more important to eradicate them. THE PRINCIPLE OBJECT OF OUR DIRECTORATE CONSISTS IN THIS: TO DEBILITATE THE PUBLIC MIND BY CRITICISM; TO LEAD IT AWAY FROM SERIOUS REFLECTIONS CALCULATED TO AROUSE RESISTANCE; TO DISTRACT THE FORCES OF THE MIND TOWARDS A SHAM FIGHT OF EMPTY ELOQUENCE.

8. In all ages the people of the world, equally with individuals, have accepted words for deeds, for THEY ARE CONTENT WITH A SHOW and rarely pause to note, in the public arena, whether promises are followed by performance. Therefore we shall establish show institutions which will give eloquent proof of their benefit to progress.

9. We shall assume to ourselves the liberal physiognomy of all parties, of all directions, and we shall give that physiognomy a VOICE IN ORATORS

WHO WILL SPEAK SO MUCH THAT THEY WILL EXHAUST THE PATIENCE OF THEIR HEARERS AND PRODUCE AN ABHORRENCE OF ORATORY.

10. IN ORDER TO PUT PUBLIC OPINION INTO OUR HANDS WE MUST BRING IT INTO A STATE OF BEWILDERMENT BY GIVING EXPRESSION FROM ALL SIDES TO SO MANY CONTRADICTORY OPINIONS AND FOR SUCH LENGTH OF TIME AS WILL SUFFICE TO MAKE THE *"GOYIM"* LOSE THEIR HEADS IN THE LABYRINTH AND COME TO SEE THAT THE BEST THING IS TO HAVE NO OPINION OF ANY KIND IN MATTERS POLITICAL, which it is not given to the public to understand, because they are understood only by him who guides the public. This is the first secret.

11. The second secret requisite for the success of our government is comprised in the following: To multiply to such an extent national failings, habits, passions, conditions of civil life, that it will be impossible for anyone to know where he is in the resulting chaos, so that the people in consequence will fail to understand one another. This measure will also serve us in another way, namely, to sow discord in all parties, to dislocate all collective forces which are still unwilling to submit to us, and to discourage any kind of personal initiative which might in any degree hinder our affair. THERE IS NOTHING MORE DANGEROUS THAN PERSONAL INITIATIVE: if it has genius behind it, such initiative can do more than can be done by millions of people among whom we have sown discord. We must so direct the education of the GOYIM communities that whenever they come upon a matter requiring initiative they may drop their hands in despairing impotence. The strain which results from freedom of actions saps the forces when it meets with the freedom of another. From this collision arise grave moral shocks, disenchantments, failures. BY ALL THESE MEANS WE SHALL SO WEAR DOWN THE "GOYIM" THAT THEY WILL BE COMPELLED TO OFFER US INTERNATIONAL POWER OF A NATURE THAT BY ITS POSITION WILL ENABLE US WITHOUT ANY VIOLENCE GRADUALLY TO ABSORB ALL THE STATE FORCES OF THE WORLD AND TO FORM A SUPER-GOVERNMENT. In place of the rulers of to-day we shall set up a bogey which will be called the Super-Government Administration. Its hands will reach out in all directions like nippers and its organization will be of such colossal dimensions that it cannot fail to subdue all the nations of the world. (League of Nations and subsequent United Nations Organization - Ed.).

PROTOCOL No. 6

1. We shall soon begin to establish huge monopolies, reservoirs of colossal riches, upon which even large fortunes of the GOYIM will depend to such an extent that they will go to the bottom together with the credit of the States on the day after the political smash ... (Compulsory superannuation, Social Security).

2. You gentlemen here present who are economists, just strike an estimate of the significance of this combination! ...

3. In every possible way we must develop the significance of our Super-Government by representing it as the Protector and Benefactor of all those who voluntarily submit to us.

4. The aristocracy of the GOYIM as a political force, is dead - We need not take it into account; but as landed proprietors they can still be harmful to us from the fact that they are self-sufficing in the resources upon which they live. It is essential therefore for us at whatever cost to deprive them of their land. This object will be best attained by increasing the burdens upon landed property - in loading lands with debts. These measures will check land-holding and keep it in a state of humble and unconditional submission.

5. The aristocrats of the GOYIM, being hereditarily incapable of contenting themselves with little, will rapidly burn up and fizzle out.

WE SHALL ENSLAVE GENTILES

6. At the same time we must intensively patronize trade and industry, but first and foremost, speculation, the part played by which is to provide a counterpoise to industry: the absence of speculative industry will multiply capital in private hands and will serve to restore agriculture by freeing the land from indebtedness to the land banks. What we want is that industry should drain off from the land both labor and capital and by means of speculation transfer into our hands all the money of the world, and thereby throw all the GOYIM into the ranks of the proletariat. Then the GOYIM will bow down before us, if for no other reason but to get the right to exist.

7. To complete the ruin of the industry of the GOYIM we shall bring to the assistance of speculation the luxury which we have developed among the GOYIM, that greedy demand for luxury which is swallowing up everything. WE SHALL RAISE THE RATE OF WAGES WHICH, HOWEVER,

WILL NOT BRING ANY ADVANTAGE TO THE WORKERS, FOR, AT THE SAME TIME, WE SHALL PRODUCE A RISE IN PRICES OF THE FIRST NECESSARIES OF LIFE, ALLEGING THAT IT ARISES FROM THE DECLINE OF AGRICULTURE AND CATTLE-BREEDING: WE SHALL FURTHER UNDERMINE ARTFULLY AND DEEPLY SOURCES OF PRODUCTION, BY ACCUSTOMING THE WORKERS TO ANARCHY AND TO DRUNKENNESS AND SIDE BY SIDE THEREWITH TAKING ALL MEASURE TO EXTIRPATE FROM THE FACE OF THE EARTH ALL THE EDUCATED FORCES OF THE *"GOYIM."*

8. IN ORDER THAT THE TRUE MEANING OF THINGS MAY NOT STRIKE THE *"GOYIM"* BEFORE THE PROPER TIME WE SHALL MASK IT UNDER AN ALLEGED ARDENT DESIRE TO SERVE THE WORKING CLASSES AND THE GREAT PRINCIPLES OF POLITICAL ECONOMY ABOUT WHICH OUR ECONOMIC THEORIES ARE CARRYING ON AN ENERGETIC PROPAGANDA.

PROTOCOL No. 7

1. The intensification of armaments, the increase of police forces - are all essential for the completion of the aforementioned plans. What we have to get at is that there should be in all the States of the world, besides ourselves, only the masses of the proletariat, a few millionaires devoted to our interests, police and soldiers.

2. Throughout all Europe, and by means of relations with Europe, in other continents also, we must create ferments, discords and hostility. Therein we gain a double advantage. In the first place we keep in check all countries, for they will know that we have the power whenever we like to create disorders or to restore order. All these countries are accustomed to see in us an indispensable force of coercion. In the second place, by our intrigues we shall tangle up all the threads which we have stretched into the cabinets of all States by means of the political, by economic treaties, or loan obligations. In order to succeed in this we must use great cunning and penetration during negotiations and agreements, but, as regards what is called the *"official language,"* we shall keep to the opposite tactics and assume the mask of honesty and complacency. In this way the peoples and governments of the GOYIM, whom we have taught to look only at the outside whatever we present to their notice, will still continue to accept us as the benefactors and saviours of the human race.

UNIVERSAL WAR

3. We must be in a position to respond to every act of opposition by war with the neighbors of that country which dares to oppose us: but if these neighbors should also venture to stand collectively together against us, then we must offer resistance by a universal war.

4. The principal factor of success in the political is the secrecy of its undertakings: the word should not agree with the deeds of the diplomat.

5. We must compel the governments of the GOYIM to take action in the direction favored by our widely conceived plan, already approaching the desired consummation, by what we shall represent as public opinion, secretly promoted by us through the means of that so-called *"Great Power"* - THE PRESS, WHICH, WITH A FEW EXCEPTIONS THAT MAY BE DISREGARDED, IS ALREADY ENTIRELY IN OUR HANDS.

6. In a word, to sum up our system of keeping the governments of the goyim in Europe in check, we shall show our strength to one of them by terrorist attempts and to all, if we allow the possibility of a general rising against us, we shall respond with the guns of America or China or Japan. (The Russo-Japanese War of 1904-1905 - Ed.).

PROTOCOL No. 8

1. We must arm ourselves with all the weapons which our opponents might employ against us. We must search out in the very finest shades of expression and the knotty points of the lexicon of law justification for those cases where we shall have to pronounce judgments that might appear abnormally audacious and unjust, for it is important that these resolutions should be set forth in expressions that shall seem to be the most exalted moral principles cast into legal form. *(Genocide Convention? U.N. Declaration of the Rights of the Child?)* Our directorate must surround itself with all these forces of civilization among which it will have to work. It will surround itself with publicists, practical jurists, administrators, diplomats and, finally, with persons prepared by a special super-educational training IN OUR SPECIAL SCHOOLS *(Rhodes Scholars? London School of Economics?)* These persons will have consonance of all the secrets of the social structure, they will know all the languages that can be made up by political alphabets and words; they will be made acquainted with the whole underside of human nature, with all its sensitive chords on which they will have to play. These chords are the cast of mind of the GOYIM, their tendencies, short-comings, vices and qualities, the

particularities of classes and conditions. Needless to say that the talented assistants of authority, of whom I speak, will be taken not from among the GOYIM, who are accustomed to perform their administrative work without giving themselves the trouble to think what its aim is, and never consider what it is needed for. The administrators of the GOYIM sign papers without reading them, (*As Margaret Thatcher signed-away British sovereignty by the Maastricht Treaty? As Australian Parliamentarians signed over 2,000 U.N. Treaties . . . unread?*) and they serve either for mercenary reasons or from ambition.

2. We shall surround our government with a whole world of economists. That is the reason why economic sciences form the principal subject of the teaching given to the Jews. Around us again will be a whole constellation of bankers, industrialists, capitalists and - THE MAIN THING - MILLIONAIRES, BECAUSE IN SUBSTANCE EVERYTHING WILL BE SETTLED BY THE QUESTION OF FIGURES.

3. For a time, until there will no longer be any risk in entrusting responsible posts in our State to our brother-Jews, we shall put them in the hands of persons whose past and reputation are such that between them and the people lies an abyss, persons who, in case of disobedience to our instructions, must face criminal charges or disappear - this in order to make them defend our interests to their last gasp.

PROTOCOL No. 9

I. In applying our principles let attention be paid to the character of the people in whose country you live and act; a general, identical application of them, until such time as the people shall have been re-educated to our pattern, cannot have success. But by approaching their application cautiously you will see that not a decade will pass before the most stubborn character will change and we shall add a new people to the ranks of those already subdued by us.

2. The words of the liberal, which are in effect the words of our masonic watchword, namely, *"Liberty, Equality, Fraternity,"* will, when we come into our kingdom, be changed by us into words no longer of a watchword, but only an expression of idealism, namely, into *"The right of liberty, the duty of equality, the ideal of brotherhood."* That is how we shall put it, - and so we shall catch the bull by the horns ... DE FACTO we have already wiped out every kind of rule except our own, although DE JURE there still remain a good many of them. Nowadays, if any States raise a protest against us it is only PRO FORMA at our discretion and by our direction, for THEIR ANTI-SEMITISM IS INDISPENSABLE TO US FOR THE MANAGEMENT

OF OUR LESSER BRETHREN. I will not enter into further explanations, for this matter has formed the subject of repeated discussions amongst us.

JEWISH SUPER-STATE

3. For us there are not checks to limit the range of our activity. Our Super-Government subsists in extra-legal conditions which are described in the accepted terminology by the energetic and forcible word - Dictatorship. I am in a position to tell you with a clear conscience that at the proper time we, the law-givers, shall execute judgment and sentence, we shall slay and we shall spare, we, as head of all our troops, are mounted on the steed of the leader. We rule by force of will, because in our hands are the fragments of a once powerful party, now vanquished by us. AND THE WEAPONS IN OUR HANDS ARE LIMITLESS AMBITIONS, BURNING GREEDINESS, MERCILESS VENGEANCE, HATREDS AND MALICE.

4. IT IS FROM US THAT THE ALL-ENGULFING TERROR PROCEEDS. WE HAVE IN OUR SERVICE PERSONS OF ALL OPINIONS, OF ALL DOCTRINES, RESTORATING MONARCHISTS, DEMAGOGUES, SOCIALISTS, COMMUNISTS, AND UTOPIAN DREAMERS OF EVERY KIND. We have harnessed them all to the task: EACH ONE OF THEM ON HIS OWN ACCOUNT IS BORING AWAY AT THE LAST REMNANTS OF AUTHORITY, IS STRIVING TO OVERTHROW ALL ESTABLISHED FORM OF ORDER. By these acts all States are in torture; they exhort to tranquility, are ready to sacrifice everything for peace: BUT WE WILL NOT GIVE THEM PEACE UNTIL THEY OPENLY ACKNOWLEDGE OUR INTERNATIONAL SUPER-GOVERNMENT, AND WITH SUBMISSIVENESS.

5. The people have raised a howl about the necessity of settling the question of Socialism by way of an international agreement. DIVISION INTO FRACTIONAL PARTIES HAS GIVEN THEM INTO OUR HANDS, FOR, IN ORDER TO CARRY ON A CONTESTED STRUGGLE ONE MUST HAVE MONEY, AND THE MONEY IS ALL IN OUR HANDS.

6. We might have reason to apprehend a union between the *"clear-sighted"* force of the GOY kings on their thrones and the *"blind"* force of the GOY mobs, but we have taken all the needful measure against any such possibility: between the one and the other force we have erected a bulwark in the shape of a mutual terror between them. In this way the blind force of the people remains our support and we, and we only, shall provide them with a leader and, of course, direct them along the road that leads to our goal.

7. In order that the hand of the blind mob may not free itself from our guiding hand, we must every now and then enter into close communion with it, if not actually in person, at any rate through some of the most trusty of our brethren. When we are acknowledged as the only authority we shall discuss with the people personally on the market, places, and we shall instruct them on questings of the political in such wise as may turn them in the direction that suits us.

8. Who is going to verify what is taught in the village schools? But what an envoy of the government or a king on his throne himself may say cannot but become immediately known to the whole State, for it will be spread abroad by the voice of the people.

9. In order to annihilate the institutions of the GOYIM before it is time we have touched them with craft and delicacy, and have taken hold of the ends of the springs which move their mechanism. These springs lay in a strict but just sense of order; we have replaced them by the chaotic license of liberalism. We have got our hands into the administration of the law, into the conduct of elections, into the press, into liberty of the person, BUT PRINCIPALLY INTO EDUCATION AND TRAINING AS BEING THE CORNERSTONES OF A FREE EXISTENCE.

CHRISTIAN YOUTH DESTROYED

10. WE HAVE FOOLED, BEMUSED AND CORRUPTED THE YOUTH OF THE "GOYIM" BY REARING THEM IN PRINCIPLES AND THEORIES WHICH ARE KNOWN TO US TO BE FALSE ALTHOUGH IT IS THAT THEY HAVE BEEN INCULCATED.

11. Above the existing laws without substantially altering them, and by merely twisting them into contradictions of interpretations, we have erected something grandiose in the way of results. These results found expression in the fact that the INTERPRETATIONS MASKED THE LAW: afterwards they entirely hid them from the eyes of the governments owing to the impossibility of making anything out of the tangled web of legislation.

12. This is the origin of the theory of course of arbitration.

13. You may say that the GOYIM will rise upon us, arms in hand, if they guess what is going on before the time comes; but in the West we have against this a manoeuvre of such appalling terror that the very stoutest hearts quail - the undergrounds, metropolitans, those subterranean corridors which, before

the time comes, will be driven under all the capitals and from whence those capitals will be blown into the air with all their organizations and archives.

PROTOCOL No. 10

1. To-day I begin with a repetition of what I said before, and I BEG YOU TO BEAR IN MIND THAT GOVERNMENTS AND PEOPLE ARE CONTENT IN THE POLITICAL WITH OUTSIDE APPEARANCES. And how, indeed, are the GOYIM to perceive the underlying meaning of things when their representatives give the best of their energies to enjoying themselves? For our policy it is of the greatest importance to take cognizance of this detail; it will be of assistance to us when we come to consider the division of authority of property, of the dwelling, of taxation *(the idea of concealed taxes,* of the reflex force of the laws. All these questions are such as ought not to be touched upon directly and openly before the people. In cases where it is indispensable to touch upon them they must not be categorically named, it must merely be declared without detailed exposition that the principles of contemporary law are acknowledged by us. The reason of keeping silence in this respect is that by not naming a principle we leave ourselves freedom of action, to drop this or that out of it without attracting notice; if they were all categorically named they would all appear to have been already given.

2. The mob cherishes a special affection and respect for the geniuses of political power and accepts all their deeds of violence with the admiring response: *"rascally, well, yes, it is rascally, but it's clever! ... a trick, if you like, but how craftily played, how magnificently done, what impudent audacity!"* ...

OUR GOAL - WORLD POWER

3. We count upon attracting all nations to the task of erecting the new fundamental structure, the project for which has been drawn up by us. This is why, before everything, it is indispensable for us to arm ourselves and to store up in ourselves that absolutely reckless audacity and irresistible might of the spirit which in the person of our active workers will break down all hindrances on our way.

4. WHEN WE HAVE ACCOMPLISHED OUR COUP D'ETAT WE SHALL SAY THEN TO THE VARIOUS PEOPLES: *"EVERYTHING HAS GONE TERRIBLY BADLY, ALL HAVE BEEN WORN OUT WITH SUFFERING. WE ARE DESTROYING THE CAUSES OF YOUR TORMENT - NATIONALITIES, FRONTIERS, DIFFERENCES*

OF COINAGES. YOU ARE AT LIBERTY, OF COURSE, TO PRONOUNCE SENTENCE UPON US, BUT CAN IT POSSIBLY BE A JUST ONE IF IT IS CONFIRMED BY YOU BEFORE YOU MAKE ANY TRIAL OF WHAT WE ARE OFFERING YOU." ... THEN WILL THE MOB EXALT US AND BEAR US UP IN THEIR HANDS IN A UNANIMOUS TRIUMPH OF HOPES AND EXPECTATIONS. VOTING, WHICH WE HAVE MADE THE INSTRUMENT WHICH WILL SET US ON THE THRONE OF THE WORLD BY TEACHING EVEN THE VERY SMALLEST UNITS OF MEMBERS OF THE HUMAN RACE TO VOTE BY MEANS OF MEETINGS AND AGREEMENTS BY GROUPS, WILL THEN HAVE SERVED ITS PURPOSES AND WILL PLAY ITS PART THEN FOR THE LAST TIME BY A UNANIMITY OF DESIRE TO MAKE CLOSE ACQUAINTANCE WITH US BEFORE CONDEMNING US.

5. TO SECURE THIS WE MUST HAVE EVERYBODY VOTE WITHOUT DISTINCTION OF CLASSES AND QUALIFICATIONS, in order to establish an absolute majority, which cannot be got from the educated propertied classes. In this way, by inculcating in all a sense of self-importance, we shall destroy among the GOYIM the importance of the family and its educational value and remove the possibility of individual minds splitting off, for the mob, handled by us, will not let them come to the front nor even give them a hearing; it is accustomed to listen to us only who pay it for obedience and attention. In this way we shall create a blind, mighty force which will never be in a position to move in any direction without the guidance of our agents set at its head by us as leaders of the mob. The people will submit to this regime because it will know that upon these leaders will depend its earnings, gratifications and the receipt of all kinds of benefits.

6. A scheme of government should come ready made from one brain, because it will never be clinched firmly if it is allowed to be split into fractional parts in the minds of many. It is allowable, therefore, for us to have cognizance of the scheme of action but not to discuss it lest we disturb its artfulness, the interdependence of its component parts, the practical force of the secret meaning of each clause. To discuss and make alterations in a labor of this kind by means of numerous votings is to impress upon it the stamp of all ratiocinations and misunderstandings which have failed to penetrate the depth and nexus of its plottings. We want our schemes to be forcible and suitably concocted. Therefore WE OUGHT NOT TO FLING THE WORK OF GENIUS OF OUR GUIDE to the fangs of the mob or even of a select company.

7. These schemes will not turn existing institutions upside down just yet. They will only effect changes in their economy and consequently in the whole combined movement of their progress, which will thus be directed along the paths laid down in our schemes.

POISON OF LIBERALISM

8. Under various names there exists in all countries approximately one and the same thing. Representation, Ministry, Senate, State Council, Legislative and Executive Corps. I need not explain to you the mechanism of the relation of these institutions to one another, because you are aware of all that; only take note of the fact that each of the above-named institutions corresponds to some important function of the State, and I would beg you to remark that the word *"important"* I apply not to the institution but to the function, consequently it is not the institutions which are important but their functions. These institutions have divided up among themselves all the functions of government - administrative, legislative, executive, wherefore they have come to operate as do the organs in the human body. If we injure one part in the machinery of State, the State falls sick, like a human body, and ... will die.

9. When we introduced into the State organism the poison of Liberalism its whole political complexion underwent a change. States have been seized with a mortal illness - blood poisoning. All that remains is to await the end of their death agony.

10. Liberalism produced Constitutional States, which took the place of what was the only safeguard of the GOYIM, namely, Despotism; and A CONSTITUTION, AS YOU WELL KNOW, IS NOTHING ELSE BUT A SCHOOL OF DISCORDS, misunderstandings, quarrels, disagreements, fruitless party agitations, party whims - in a word, a school of everything that serves to destroy the personality of State activity. THE TRIBUNE OF THE "TALKERIES" HAS, NO LESS EFFECTIVELY THAN THE PRESS, CONDEMNED THE RULERS TO INACTIVITY AND IMPOTENCE, and thereby rendered them useless and superfluous, for which reason indeed they have been in many countries deposed. THEN IT WAS THAT THE ERA OF REPUBLICS BECOME POSSIBLE OF REALIZATION; AND THEN IT WAS THAT WE REPLACED THE RULER BY A CARICATURE OF A GOVERNMENT - BY A PRESIDENT, TAKEN FROM THE MOB, FROM THE MIDST OF OUR PUPPET CREATURES, OR SLAVES. This was the foundation of the mine which we have laid under the GOY people, I should rather say, under the GOY peoples.

WE NAME PRESIDENTS

11. In the near future we shall establish the responsibility of presidents.

12. By that time we shall be in a position to disregard forms in carrying through matters for which our impersonal puppet will be responsible. What do we care if the ranks of those striving for power should be thinned, if there should arise a deadlock from the impossibility of finding presidents, a deadlock which will finally disorganize the country? ...

13. In order that our scheme may produce this result we shall arrange elections in favor of such presidents as have in their past some dark, undiscovered stain, some "Panama" or other - then they will be trustworthy agents for the accomplishment of our plans out of fear of revelations and from the natural desire of everyone who has attained power, namely, the retention of the privileges, advantages and honor connected with the office of president. The chamber of deputies will provide cover for, will protect, will elect presidents, but we shall take from it the right to propose new, or make changes in existing laws, for this right will be given by us to the responsible president, a puppet in our hands. Naturally, the authority of the presidents will then become a target for every possible form of attack, but we shall provide him with a means of self-defense in the right of an appeal to the people, for the decision of the people over the heads of their representatives, that is to say, an appeal to that same blind slave of ours - the majority of the mob. Independently of this we shall invest the president with the right of declaring a state of war. We shall justify this last right on the ground that the president as chief of the whole army of the country must have it at his disposal, in case of need for the defense of the new republican constitution, the right to defend which will belong to him as the responsible representative of this constitution. (*Iran? Grenada? Kuwait? Iraq? Panama? Somalia? Bosnia? Kosovo? Indonesia?*)

14. It is easy to understand that in these conditions the key of the shrine will lie in our hands, and no one outside ourselves will any longer direct the force of legislation.

15. Besides this we shall, with the introduction of the new republican constitution, take from the Chamber the right of interpolation on government measures, on the pretext of preserving political secrecy, and, further, we shall by the new constitution reduce the number of representatives to a minimum, thereby proportionately reducing political passions and the passion for politics. If, however, they should, which is hardly to be expected, burst into flame, even in this minimum, we shall nullify them by a stirring appeal and a reference to the majority of the whole people ... Upon the president will depend the

appointment of presidents and vice-presidents of the Chamber and the Senate. Instead of constant sessions of Parliaments we shall reduce their sittings to a few months. Moreover, the president, as chief of the executive power, will have the right to summon and dissolve Parliament, and, in the latter case, to prolong the time for the appointment of a new parliamentary assembly. But in order that the consequences of all these acts which in substance are illegal, should not, prematurely for our plans, fall upon the responsibility established by us of the president, WE SHALL INSTIGATE MINISTERS AND OTHER OFFICIALS OF THE HIGHER ADMINISTRATION ABOUT THE PRESIDENT TO EVADE HIS DISPOSITIONS BY TAKING MEASURES OF THEIR OWN, for doing which they will be made the scapegoats in his place ... This part we especially recommend to be given to be played by the Senate, the Council of State, or the Council of Ministers, but not to an individual official.

16. The president will, at our discretion, interpret the sense of such of the existing laws as admit of various interpretation; he will further annul them when we indicate to him the necessity to do so, besides this, he will have the right to propose temporary laws, and even new departures in the government constitutional working, the pretext both for the one and the other being the requirements for the supreme welfare of the State. *(Presidential Decrees such as F.D.R. employed to debase the US dollar and steal the gold and to place the U.S. under a permanent State of Emergency and War against its own citizens?)*

WE SHALL DESTROY

17. By such measure we shall obtain the power of destroying little by little, step by step, all that at the outset when we enter on our rights, we are compelled to introduce into the constitutions of States to prepare for the transition to an imperceptible abolition of every kind of constitution, and then the time is come to turn every form of government into OUR DESPOTISM.

18. The recognition of our despot may also come before the destruction of the constitution; the moment for this recognition will come when the peoples, utterly wearied by the irregularities and incompetence - a matter which we shall arrange for - of their rulers, will clamor: *"Away with them and give us one king over all the earth who will unite us and annihilate the causes of disorders - frontiers, nationalities, religions, State debts - who will give us peace and quiet which we cannot find under our rulers and representatives."*

19. But you yourselves perfectly well know that TO PRODUCE THE POSSIBILITY OF THE EXPRESSION OF SUCH WISHES BY ALL THE NATIONS IT IS INDISPENSABLE TO TROUBLE IN ALL

COUNTRIES THE PEOPLE'S RELATIONS WITH THEIR GOVERNMENTS SO AS TO UTTERLY EXHAUST HUMANITY WITH DISSENSION, HATRED, STRUGGLE, ENVY AND EVEN BY THE USE OF TORTURE, BY STARVATION, BY THE INOCULATION OF DISEASES, BY WANT, SO THAT THE "GOYIM" SEE NO OTHER ISSUE THAN TO TAKE REFUGE IN OUR COMPLETE SOVEREIGNTY IN MONEY AND IN ALL ELSE.

20. But if we give the nations of the world a breathing space the moment we long for is hardly likely ever to arrive.

PROTOCOL No. II

1. The State Council has been, as it were, the emphatic expression of the authority of the ruler: it will be, as the *"show"* part of the Legislative Corps, what may be called the editorial committee of the laws and decrees of the ruler.

2. This, then, is the program of the new constitution. We shall make Law, Right and Justice (1) in the guise of proposals to the Legislative Corps, (2) by decrees of the president under the guise of general regulations, of orders of the Senate and of resolutions of the State Council in the guise of ministerial orders, (3) and in case a suitable occasion should arise - in the form of a revolution in the State.

3. Having established approximately the MODUS AGENDI we will occupy ourselves with details of those combinations by which we have still to complete the revolution in the course of the machinery of State in the direction already indicated. By these combinations I mean the freedom of the Press, the right of association, freedom of conscience, the voting principle, and many another that must disappear for ever from the memory of man, or undergo a radical alteration the day after the promulgation of the new constitution. It is only at the moment that we shall be able at once to announce all our orders, for, afterwards, every noticeable alteration will be dangerous, for the following reasons: if this alteration be brought in with harsh severity and in a sense of severity and limitations, it may lead to a feeling of despair caused by fear of new alterations in the same direction; if, on the other hand, it be brought in a sense of further indulgences it will be said that we have recognized our own wrong-doing and this will destroy the prestige of the infallibility of our authority, or else it will be said that we have become alarmed and are compelled to show a yielding disposition, for which we shall get no thanks because it will be supposed to be compulsory ... Both the one and the other are injurious to the prestige of the new constitution. What we want is that from the first moment of its promulgation, while the peoples of the world are still

106

stunned by the accomplished fact of the revolution, still in a condition of terror and uncertainty, they should recognize once for all that we are so strong, so inexpugnable, so super-abundantly filled with power, that in no case shall we take any account of them, and so far from paying any attention to their opinions or wishes, we are ready and able to crush with irresistible power all expression or manifestation thereof at every moment and in every place, that we have seized at once everything we wanted and shall in no case divide our power with them ... Then in fear and trembling they will close their eyes to everything, and be content to await what will be the end of it all.

WE ARE WOLVES

4. The GOYIM are a flock of sheep, and we are their wolves. And you know what happens when the wolves get hold of the flock? ....

5. There is another reason also why they will close their eyes: for we shall keep promising them to give back all the liberties we have taken away as soon as we have quelled the enemies of peace and tamed all parties ....

6. It is not worth to say anything about how long a time they will be kept waiting for this return of their liberties ....

7. For what purpose then have we invented this whole policy and insinuated it into the minds of the GOY without giving them any chance to examine its underlying meaning? For what, indeed, if not in order to obtain in a roundabout way what is for our scattered tribe unattainable by the direct road? It is this which has served as the basis for our organization of SECRET MASONRY WHICH IS NOT KNOWN TO, AND AIMS WHICH ARE NOT EVEN SO MUCH AS SUSPECTED BY, THESE *"GOY"* CATTLE, ATTRACTED BY US INTO THE *"SHOW"* ARMY OF MASONIC LODGES IN ORDER TO THROW DUST IN THE EYES OF THEIR FELLOWS.

8. God has granted to us, His Chosen People, the gift of the dispersion, and in this which appears in all eyes to be our weakness, has come forth all our strength, which has now brought us to the threshold of sovereignty over all the world.

9. There now remains not much more for us to build up upon the foundation we have laid.

PROTOCOL No. 12

1. The word *"freedom,"* which can be interpreted in various ways, is defined by us as follows -

2. Freedom is the right to do what which the law allows. This interpretation of the word will at the proper time be of service to us, because all freedom will thus be in our hands, since the laws will abolish or create only that which is desirable for us according to the aforesaid program.

3. We shall deal with the press in the following way: what is the part played by the press to-day? It serves to excite and inflame those passions which are needed for our purpose or else it serves selfish ends of parties. It is often vapid, unjust, mendacious, and the majority of the public have not the slightest idea what ends the press really serves. We shall saddle and bridle it with a tight curb: we shall do the same also with all productions of the printing press, for where would be the sense of getting rid of the attacks of the press if we remain targets for pamphlets and books? The produce of publicity, which nowadays is a source of heavy expense owing to the necessity of censoring it, will be turned by us into a very lucrative source of income to our State: we shall lay on it a special stamp tax and require deposits of caution-money before permitting the establishment of any organ of the press or of printing offices; these will then have to guarantee our government against any kind of attack on the part of the press. For any attempt to attack us, if such still be possible, we shall inflict fines without mercy. Such measures as stamp tax, deposit of caution-money and fines secured by these deposits, will bring in a huge income to the government. It is true that party organs might not spare money for the sake of publicity, but these we shall shut up at the second attack upon us. No one shall with impunity lay a finger on the aureole of our government infallibility. The pretext for stopping any publication will be the alleged plea that it is agitating the public mind without occasion or justification. I BEG YOU TO NOTE THAT AMONG THOSE MAKING ATTACKS UPON US WILL ALSO BE ORGANS ESTABLISHED BY US, BUT THEY WILL ATTACK EXCLUSIVELY POINTS THAT WE HAVE PRE-DETERMINED TO ALTER.

WE CONTROL THE PRESS

4. NOT A SINGLE ANNOUNCEMENT WILL REACH THE PUBLIC WITHOUT OUR CONTROL. Even now this is already being attained by us inasmuch as all news items are received by a few agencies, in whose offices they are focused from all parts of the world. These agencies will then be already entirely ours and will give publicity only to what we dictate to them.

5. If already now we have contrived to possess ourselves of the minds of the GOY communities to such an extent the they all come near looking upon the events of the world through the colored glasses of those spectacles we are setting astride their noses; if already now there is not a single State where there exist for us any barriers to admittance into what GOY stupidity calls State secrets: what will our positions be then, when we shall be acknowledged supreme lords of the world in the person of our king of all the world ....

6. Let us turn again to the FUTURE OF THE PRINTING PRESS. Every one desirous of being a publisher, librarian, or printer, will be obliged to provide himself with the diploma instituted therefore, which, in case of any fault, will be immediately impounded. With such measures THE INSTRUMENT OF THOUGHT WILL BECOME AN EDUCATIVE MEANS ON THE HANDS OF OUR GOVERNMENT, WHICH WILL NO LONGER ALLOW THE MASS OF THE NATION TO BE LED ASTRAY IN BY-WAYS AND FANTASIES ABOUT THE BLESSINGS OF PROGRESS. Is there any one of us who does not know that these phantom blessings are the direct roads to foolish imaginings which give birth to anarchical relations of men among themselves and towards authority, because progress, or rather the idea of progress, has introduced the conception of every kind of emancipation, but has failed to establish its limits .... All the so-called liberals are anarchists, if not in fact, at any rate in thought. Every one of them in hunting after phantoms of freedom, and falling exclusively into license, that is, into the anarchy of protest for the sake of protest....

FREE PRESS DESTROYED

7. We turn to the periodical press. We shall impose on it, as on all printed matter, stamp taxes per sheet and deposits of caution-money, and books of less than 30 sheets will pay double. We shall reckon them as pamphlets in order, on the one hand, to reduce the number of magazines, which are the worst form of printed poison, and, on the other, in order that this measure may force writers into such lengthy productions that they will be little read, especially as they will be costly. At the same time what we shall publish ourselves to influence mental development in the direction laid down for our profit will be cheap and will be read voraciously. The tax will bring vapid literary ambitions within bounds and the liability to penalties will make literary men dependent upon us. And if there should be any found who are desirous of writing against us, they will not find any person eager to print their productions. Before accepting any production for publication in print, the publisher or printer will have to apply to the authorities for permission to do so. Thus we shall know beforehand of all tricks preparing against us and shall nullify them by getting ahead with explanations on the subject treated of.

8. Literature and journalism are two of the most important educative forces, and therefore our government will become proprietor of the majority of the journals. This will neutralize the injurious influence of the privately-owned press and will put us in possession of a tremendous influence upon the public mind .... If we give permits for ten journals, we shall ourselves found thirty, and so on in the same proportion. This, however, must in no wise be suspected by the public. For which reason all journals published by us will be of the most opposite, in appearance, tendencies and opinions, thereby creating confidence in us and bringing over to us quite unsuspicious opponents, who will thus fall into our trap and be rendered harmless.

9. In the front rank will stand organs of an official character. They will always stand guard over our interests, and therefore their influence will be comparatively insignificant.

10. In the second rank will be the semi-official organs, whose part it will be to attack the tepid and indifferent.

11. In the third rank we shall set up our own, to all appearance, opposition, which, in at least one of its organs, will present what looks like the very antipodes to us. Our real opponents at heart will accept this simulated opposition as their own and will show us their cards.

12. All our newspapers will be of all possible complexions -- aristocratic, republican, revolutionary, even anarchical - for so long, of course, as the constitution exists .... Like the Indian idol *"Vishnu"* they will have a hundred hands, and every one of them will have a finger on any one of the public opinions as required. When a pulse quickens these hands will lead opinion in the direction of our aims, for an excited patient loses all power of judgment and easily yields to suggestion. Those fools who will think they are repeating the opinion of a newspaper of their own camp will be repeating our opinion or any opinion that seems desirable for us. In the vain belief that they are following the organ of their party they will, in fact, follow the flag which we hang out for them.

13. In order to direct our newspaper militia in this sense we must take special and minute care in organizing this matter. Under the title of central department of the press we shall institute literary gatherings at which our agents will without attracting attention issue the orders and watchwords of the day. By discussing and controverting, but always superficially, without touching the essence of the matter, our organs will carry on a sham fight fusillade with the official newspapers solely for the purpose of giving occasion for us to

express ourselves more fully than could well be done from the outset in official announcements, whenever, of course, that is to our advantage.

14. THESE ATTACKS UPON US WILL ALSO SERVE ANOTHER PURPOSE, NAMELY, THAT OUR SUBJECTS WILL BE CONVINCED TO THE EXISTENCE OF FULL FREEDOM OF SPEECH AND SO GIVE OUR AGENTS AN OCCASION TO AFFIRM THAT ALL ORGANS WHICH OPPOSE US ARE EMPTY BABBLERS, since they are incapable of finding any substantial objections to our orders.

ONLY LIES PRINTED

15. Methods of organization like these, imperceptible to the public eye but absolutely sure, are the best calculated to succeed in bringing the attention and the confidence of the public to the side of our government. Thanks to such methods we shall be in a position as from time to time may be required, to excite or to tranquillize the public mind on political questions, to persuade or to confuse, printing now truth, now lies, facts or their contradictions, according as they may be well or ill received, always very cautiously feeling our ground before stepping upon it .... WE SHALL HAVE A SURE TRIUMPH OVER OUR OPPONENTS SINCE THEY WILL NOT HAVE AT THEIR DISPOSITION ORGANS OF THE PRESS IN WHICH THEY CAN GIVE FULL AND FINAL EXPRESSION TO THEIR VIEWS owing to the aforesaid methods of dealing with the press. We shall not even need to refute them except very superficially.

16. Trial shots like these, fired by us in the third rank of our press, in case of need, will be energetically refuted by us in our semi-official organs.

17. Even nowadays, already, to take only the French press, there are forms which reveal masonic solidarity in acting on the watchword: all organs of the press are bound together by professional secrecy; like the augurs of old, not one of their numbers will give away the secret of his sources of information unless it be resolved to make announcement of them. Not one journalist will venture to betray this secret, for not one of them is ever admitted to practice literature unless his whole past has some disgraceful sore or other .... These sores would be immediately revealed. So long as they remain the secret of a few the prestige of the journalist attacks the majority of the country - the mob follow after him with enthusiasm.

18. Our calculations are especially extended to the provinces. It is indispensable for us to inflame there those hopes and impulses with which we

could at any moment fall upon the capital, and we shall represent to the capitals that these expressions are the independent hopes and impulses of the provinces. Naturally, the source of them will be always one and the same - ours. WHAT WE NEED IS THAT, UNTIL SUCH TIME AS WE ARE IN THE PLENITUDE POWER, THE CAPITALS SHOULD FIND THEMSELVES STIFLED BY THE PROVINCIAL OPINION OF THE NATIONS, I.E., OF A MAJORITY ARRANGED BY OUR AGENTUR. What we need is that at the psychological moment the capitals should not be in a position to discuss an accomplished fact for the simple reason, if for no other, that it has been accepted by the public opinion of a majority in the provinces.

19. WHEN WE ARE IN THE PERIOD OF THE NEW REGIME TRANSITIONAL TO THAT OF OUR ASSUMPTION OF FULL SOVEREIGNTY WE MUST NOT ADMIT ANY REVELATION BY THE PRESS OF ANY FORM OF PUBLIC DISHONESTY; IT IS NECESSARY THAT THE NEW REGIME SHOULD BE THOUGHT TO HAVE SO PERFECTLY CONTENDED EVERYBODY THAT EVEN CRIMINALITY HAS DISAPPEARED ... Cases of the manifestation of criminality should remain known only to their victims and to chance witnesses - no more.

PROTOCOL No. 13

1. The need for daily bread forces the GOYIM to keep silence and be our humble servants. Agents taken on to our press from among the GOYIM will at our orders discuss anything which it is inconvenient for us to issue directly in official documents, and we meanwhile, quietly amid the din of the discussion so raised, shall simply take and carry through such measures as we wish and then offer them to the public as an accomplished fact. No one will dare to demand the abrogation of a matter once settled, all the more so as it will be represented as an improvement ... And immediately the press will distract the current of thought towards, new questions, (*have we not trained people always to be seeking something new?*). Into the discussions of these new questions will throw themselves those of the brainless dispensers of fortunes who are not able even now to understand that they have not the remotest conception about the matters which they undertake to discuss. Questions of the political are unattainable for any save those who have guided it already for many ages, the creators.

2. From all this you will see that in securing the opinion of the mob we are only facilitating the working of our machinery, and you may remark that it is not for actions but for words issued by us on this or that question that we

seem to seek approval. We are constantly making public declaration that we are guided in all our undertakings by the hope, joined to the conviction, that we are serving the common weal.

WE DECEIVE WORKERS

3. In order to distract people who may be too troublesome from discussions of questions of the political we are now putting forward what we allege to be new questions of the political, namely, questions of industry. In this sphere let them discuss themselves silly! The masses are agreed to remain inactive, to take a rest from what they suppose to be political *(which we trained them to in order to use them as a means of combating the GOY governments)* only on condition of being found new employments, in which we are prescribing them something that looks like the same political object. In order that the masses themselves may not guess what they are about WE FURTHER DISTRACT THEM WITH AMUSEMENTS, GAMES, PASTIMES, PASSIONS, PEOPLE'S PALACES .... SOON WE SHALL BEGIN THROUGH THE PRESS TO PROPOSE COMPETITIONS IN ART, IN SPORT IN ALL KINDS: these interests will finally distract their minds from questions in which we should find ourselves compelled to oppose them. Growing more and more unaccustomed to reflect and form any opinions of their own, people will begin to talk in the same tone as we because we alone shall be offering them new directions for thought ... of course through such persons as will not be suspected of solidarity with us.

4. The part played by the liberals, utopian dreamers, will be finally played out when our government is acknowledged. Till such time they will continue to do us good service. Therefore we shall continue to direct their minds to all sorts of vain conceptions of fantastic theories, new and apparently progressive: for have we not with complete success turned the brainless heads of the GOYIM with progress, till there is not among the GOYIM one mind able to perceive that under this word lies a departure from truth in all cases where it is not a question of material inventions, for truth is one, and in it there is no place for progress. Progress, like a fallacious idea, serves to obscure truth so that none may know it except us, the Chosen of God, its guardians.

5. When, we come into our kingdom our orators will expound great problems which have turned humanity upside down in order to bring it at the end under our beneficent rule.

6. Who will ever suspect then that ALL THESE PEOPLES WERE STAGE-MANAGED BY US ACCORDING TO A POLITICAL PLAN WHICH

NO ONE HAS SO MUCH AS GUESSED AT IN THE COURSE OF MANY CENTURIES?

PROTOCOL No. 14

1. When we come into our kingdom it will be undesirable for us that there should exist any other religion than ours of the One God with whom our destiny is bound up by our position as the Chosen People and through whom our same destiny is united with the destinies of the world. We must therefore sweep away all other forms of belief. If this gives birth to the atheists whom we see to-day, it will not, being only a transitional stage, interfere with our views, but will serve as a warning for those generations which will hearken to our preaching of the religion of Moses, that, by its stable and thoroughly elaborated system has brought all the peoples of the world into subjection to us. Therein we shall emphasize its mystical right, on which, as we shall say, all its educative power is based .... Then at every possible opportunity we shall publish articles in which we shall make comparisons between our beneficent rule and those of past ages. The blessing of tranquillity, though it be a tranquillity forcibly brought about by centuries of agitation, will throw into higher relief the benefits to which we shall point. The errors of the GOYIM governments will be depicted by us in the most vivid hues. We shall implant such an abhorrence of them that the peoples will prefer tranquillity in a state of serfdom to those rights of vaunted freedom which have tortured humanity and exhausted the very sources of human existence, sources which have been exploited by a mob of rascally adventurers who know not what they do .... USELESS CHANGES OF FORMS OF GOVERNMENT TO WHICH WE INSTIGATED THE "GOYIM" WHEN WE WERE UNDERMINING THEIR STATE STRUCTURES, WILL HAVE SO WEARIED THE PEOPLES BY THAT TIME THAT THEY WILL PREFER TO SUFFER ANYTHING UNDER US RATHER THAN RUN THE RISK OF ENDURING AGAIN ALL THE AGITATIONS AND MISERIES THEY HAVE GONE THROUGH.

WE SHALL FORBID CHRIST

2. At the same time we shall not omit to emphasize the historical mistakes of the GOY governments which have tormented humanity for so many centuries by their lack of understanding of everything that constitutes the true good of humanity in their chase after fantastic schemes of social blessings, and have never noticed that these schemes kept on producing a worse and never a better state of the universal relations which are the basis of human life ...

3. The whole force of our principles and methods will lie in the fact that we shall present them and expound them as a splendid contrast to the dead and decomposed old order of things in social life.

4. Our philosophers will discuss all the shortcomings of the various beliefs of the *"GOYIM,"* BUT NO ONE WILL EVER BRING UNDER DISCUSSION OUR FAITH FROM ITS TRUE POINT OF VIEW SINCE THIS WILL BE FULLY LEARNED BY NONE SAVE OURS WHO WILL NEVER DARE TO BETRAY ITS SECRETS.

5. IN COUNTRIES KNOWN AS PROGRESSIVE AND ENLIGHTENED WE HAVE CREATED A SENSELESS, FILTHY, ABOMINABLE LITERATURE. For some time after our entrance to power we shall continue to encourage its existence in order to provide a telling relief by contrast to the speeches, party program, which will be distributed from exalted quarters of ours .... Our wise men, trained to become leaders of the GOYIM, will compose speeches, projects, memoirs, articles, which will be used by us to influence the minds of the GOYIM, directing them towards such understanding and forms of knowledge as have been determined by us.

PROTOCOL No. 15

1. When we at last definitely come into our kingdom by the aid of COUPS D'ETAT prepared everywhere for one and the same day, after definitely acknowledged *(and not a little time will pass before that comes about, perhaps even a whole century)* we shall make it our task to see that against us such things as plots shall no longer exist. With this purpose we shall slay without mercy all who take arms *(in hand, like Waco? Randy Weaver? Port Arthur? Oklahoma?)* to oppose our coming into our kingdom. Every kind of new institution of anything like a secret society will also be punished with death; those of them which are now in existence, are known to us, serve us and have served us, we shall disband and send into exile to continents far removed from Europe. IN THIS WAY WE SHALL PROCEED WITH THOSE *"GOY"* MASONS WHO KNOW TOO MUCH; such of these as we may for some reason spare will be kept in constant fear of exile. We shall promulgate a law making all former members of secret societies liable to exile from Europe as the center of rule.

2. Resolutions of our government will be final, without appeal.

3. In the GOY societies, in which we have planted and deeply rooted discord and protestantism, the only possible way of restoring order is to employ

merciless measures that prove the direct force of authority: no regard must be paid to the victims who fall, they suffer for the well-being of the future. The attainment of that well-being, even at the expense of sacrifices, is the duty of any kind of government that acknowledges as justification for its existence not only its privileges but its obligations. The principal guarantee of stability of rule is to confirm the aureole of power, and this aureole is attained only by such a majestic inflexibility of might as shall carry on its face the emblems of inviolability from mystical causes - from the choice of God. SUCH WAS, UNTIL RECENT TIMES, THE RUSSIAN AUTOCRACY, THE ONE AND ONLY SERIOUS FOE WE HAD IN THE WORLD, WITHOUT COUNTING THE PAPACY. Bear in mind the example when Italy, drenched with blood, never touched a hair of the head of Sulla who had poured forth that blood: Sulla enjoyed an apotheosis for his might in him, but his intrepid return to Italy ringed him round with inviolability. The people do not lay a finger on him who hypnotizes them by his daring and strength of mind.

SECRET SOCIETIES

4. Meantime, however, until we come into our kingdom, we shall act in the contrary way: we shall create and multiply free masonic lodges in all the countries of the world, absorb into them all who may become or who are prominent in public activity, for these lodges we shall find our principal intelligence office and means of influence. All these lodges we shall bring under one central administration, known to us alone and to all others absolutely unknown, which will be composed of our learned elders. The lodges will have their representatives who will serve to screen the above-mentioned administration of MASONRY and from whom will issue the watchword and program. In these lodges we shall tie together the knot which binds together all revolutionary and liberal elements. Their composition will be made up of all strata of society. The most secret political plots will be known to us and fall under our guiding hands on the very day of their conception. AMONG THE MEMBERS OF THESE LODGES WILL BE ALMOST ALL THE AGENTS OF INTERNATIONAL AND NATIONAL POLICE since their service is for us irreplaceable in the respect that the police is in a position not only to use its own particular measures with the insubordinate, but also to screen our activities and provide pretexts for discontents, ET CETERA.

5. The class of people who most willingly enter into secret societies are those who live by their wits, careerists, and in general people, mostly light-minded, with whom we shall have no difficulty in dealing and in using to wind up the mechanism of the machine devised by us. If this world grows agitated the meaning of that will be that we have had to stir up in order to break up its too

great solidarity. BUT IF THERE SHOULD ARISE IN ITS MIDST A PLOT, THEN AT THE HEAD OF THAT PLOT WILL BE NO OTHER THAN ONE OF OUR MOST TRUSTED SERVANTS. It is natural that we and no other should lead MASONIC activities, for we know whither we are leading, we know the final goal of every form of activity whereas the GOYIM have knowledge of nothing, not even of the immediate effect of action; they put before themselves, usually, the momentary reckoning of the satisfaction of their self-opinion in the accomplishment of their thought without even remarking that the very conception never belonged to their initiative but to our instigation of their thought ...

GENTILES ARE STUPID

6. The GOYIM enter the lodges out of curiosity or in the hope by their means to get a nibble at the public pie, and some of them in order to obtain a hearing before the public for their impracticable and groundless fantasies: they thirst for the emotion of success and applause, of which we are remarkably generous. And the reason why we give them this success is to make use of the high conceit of themselves to which it gives birth, for that insensibly disposes them to assimulate our suggestions without being on their guard against them in the fullness of their confidence that it is their own infallibility which is giving utterance to their own thoughts and that it is impossible for them to borrow those of others .... You cannot imagine to what extent the wisest of the GOYIM can be brought to a state of unconscious naivete in the presence of this condition of high conceit of themselves, and at the same time how easy it is to take the heart out of them by the slightest ill-success, though it be nothing more than the stoppage of the applause they had, and to reduce them to a slavish submission for the sake of winning a renewal of success .... BY SO MUCH AS OURS DISREGARD SUCCESS IF ONLY THEY CAN CARRY THROUGH THEIR PLANS, BY SO MUCH THE *"GOYIM"* ARE WILLING TO SACRIFICE ANY PLANS ONLY TO HAVE SUCCESS. This psychology of theirs materially facilitates for us the task of setting them in the required direction. These tigers in appearance have the souls of sheep and the wind blows freely through their heads. We have set them on the hobby-horse of an idea about the absorption of individuality by the symbolic unit of COLLECTIVISM .... They have never yet and they never will have the sense to reflect that this hobby-horse is a manifest violation of the most important law of nature, which has established from the very creation of the world one unit unlike another and precisely for the purpose of instituting individuality ....

7. If we have been able to bring them to such a pitch of stupid blindness is it not a proof, and an amazingly clear proof, of the degree to which the mind of

the GOYIM is undeveloped in comparison with our mind? This it is, mainly, which guarantees our success.

GENTILES ARE CATTLE

8. And how far-seeing were our learned elders in ancient times when they said that to attain a serious end it behooves not to stop at any means or to count the victims sacrificed for the sake of that end .... We have not counted the victims of the seed of the GOY cattle, though we have sacrificed many of our own, but for that we have now already given them such a position on the earth as they could not even have dreamed of. The comparatively small numbers of the victims from the number of ours have preserved our nationality from destruction.

9. Death is the inevitable end for all. It is better to bring that end nearer to those who hinder our affairs than to ourselves, to the founders of this affair. WE EXECUTE MASONS IN SUCH WISE THAT NONE SAVE THE BROTHERHOOD CAN EVER HAVE A SUSPICION OF IT, NOT EVEN THE VICTIMS THEMSELVES OF OUR DEATH SENTENCE, THEY ALL DIE WHEN REQUIRED AS IF FROM A NORMAL KIND OF ILLNESS ..... Knowing this, even the brotherhood in its turn dare not protest. By such methods we have plucked out of the midst of MASONRY the very root of protest against our disposition. While preaching liberalism to the GOY we at the same time keep our own people and our agents in a state of unquestioning submission.

10. Under our influence the execution of the laws of the GOYIM has been reduced to a minimum. The prestige of the law has been exploded by the liberal interpretations introduced into this sphere. In the most important and fundamental affairs and questions, JUDGES DECIDE AS WE DICTATE TO THEM, see matters in the light wherewith we enfold them for the administration of the GOYIM, of course, through persons who are our tools though we do not appear to have anything in common with them - by newspaper opinion or by other means .... Even senators and the higher administration accept our counsels. The purely brute mind of the GOYIM is incapable of use for analysis and observation, and still more for the foreseeing whither a certain manner of setting a question may tend.

11. In this difference in capacity for thought between the GOYIM and ourselves may be clearly discerned the seal of our position as the Chosen People and of our higher quality of humanness, in contradistinction to the brute mind of the GOYIM. Their eyes are open, but see nothing before them

and do not invent *(unless perhaps, material things)*. From this it is plain that nature herself has destined us to guide and rule the world.

WE DEMAND SUBMISSION

12. When comes the time of our overt rule, the time to manifest its blessing, we shall remake all legislatures, all our laws will be brief, plain, stable, without any kind of interpretations, so that anyone will be in a position to know them perfectly. The main feature which will run right through them is submission to orders, and this principle will be carried to a grandiose height. Every abuse will then disappear in consequence of the responsibility of all down to the lowest unit before the higher authority of the representative of power. Abuses of power subordinate to this last instance will be so mercilessly punished that none will be found anxious to try experiments with their own powers. We shall follow up jealously every action of the administration on which depends the smooth running of the machinery of the State, for slackness in this produces slackness everywhere; not a single case of illegality or abuse of power will be left without exemplary punishment.

13. Concealment of guilt, connivance between those in the service of the administration - all this kind of evil will disappear after the very first examples of severe punishment. The aureole of our power demands suitable, that is, cruel, punishments for the slightest infringement, for the sake of gain, of its supreme prestige. The sufferer, though his punishment may exceed his fault, will count as a soldier falling on the administrative field of battle in the interests of authority, principle and law, which do not permit that any of those who hold the reins of the public coach should turn aside from the public highway to their own private paths. FOR EXAMPLES OUR JUDGES WILL KNOW THAT WHENEVER THEY FEEL DISPOSED TO PLUME THEMSELVES ON FOOLISH CLEMENCY THEY ARE VIOLATING THE LAW OF JUSTICE WHICH IS INSTITUTED FOR THE EXEMPLARY EDIFICATION OF MEN BY PENALTIES FOR LAPSES AND NOT FOR DISPLAY OF THE SPIRITUAL QUALITIES OF THE JUDGES .... Such qualities it is proper to show in private life, but not in a public square which is the educational basis of human life.

14. Our legal staff will serve not beyond the age of 55, firstly because old men more obstinately hold to prejudiced opinions, and are less capable of submitting to new directions, and secondly because this will give us the possibility by this measure of securing elasticity in the changing of staff, which will thus the more easily bend under our pressure: he who wishes to keep his place will have to give blind obedience to deserve it. In general, our judges will be elected by us only from among those who thoroughly understand that the

part they have to play is to punish and apply laws and not to dream about the manifestations of liberalism at the expense of the educational scheme of the State, as the GOYIM in these days imagine it to be .... This method of shuffling the staff will serve also to explode any collective solidarity of those in the same service and will bind all to the interests of the government upon which their fate will depend. The young generation of judges will be trained in certain views regarding the inadmissibility of any abuses that might disturb the established order of our subjects among themselves.

15. In these days the judges of the GOYIM create indulgences to every kind of crimes, not having a just understanding of their office, because the rulers of the present age in appointing judges to office take no care to inculcate in them a sense of duty and consciousness of the matter which is demanded of them. As a brute beast lets out its young in search of prey, so do the GOYIM give to them for what purpose such place was created. This is the reason why their governments are being ruined by their own forces through the acts of their own administration.

16. Let us borrow from the example of the results of these actions yet another lesson for our government.

17. We shall root out liberalism from all the important strategic posts of our government on which depends the training of subordinates for our State structure. Such posts will fall exclusively to those who have been trained by us for administrative rule. To the possible objection that the retirement of old servants will cost the Treasury heavily, I reply, firstly, they will be provided with some private service in place of what they lose, and, secondly, I have to remark that all the money in the world will be concentrated in our hands, consequently it is not our government that has to fear expense.

WE SHALL BE CRUEL

18. Our absolutism will in all things be logically consecutive and therefore in each one of its decrees our supreme will must be respected and unquestionably fulfilled: it will ignore all murmurs, all discontents of every kind and will destroy to the root every kind of manifestation of them in act by punishment of an exemplary character.

19. We shall abolish the right of appeal, which will be transferred exclusively to our disposal - to the cognizance of him who rules, for we must not allow the conception among the people of a thought that there could be such a thing as a decision that is not right of judges set up by us. If, however, anything like this

should occur, we shall ourselves quash the decision, but inflict therewith such exemplary punishment on the judge for lack of understanding of his duty and the purpose of his appointment as will prevent a repetition of such cases .... I repeat that it must be born in mind that we shall know every step of our administration which only needs to be closely watched for the people to be content with us, for it has the right to demand from a good government a good official.

20. OUR GOVERNMENT WILL HAVE THE APPEARANCE OF A PATRIARCHAL PATERNAL GUARDIANSHIP ON THE PART OF OUR RULER. Our own nation and our subjects will discern in his person a father caring for their every need, their every act, their every interrelation as subjects one with another, as well as their relations to the ruler. They will then be so thoroughly imbued with the thought that it is impossible for them to dispense with this wardship and guidance, if they wish to live in peace and quiet, THAT THEY WILL ACKNOWLEDGE THE AUTOCRACY OF OUR RULER WITH A DEVOTION BORDERING ON "APOTHEOSIS," especially when they are convinced that those whom we set up do not put their own in place of authority, but only blindly execute his dictates. They will be rejoiced that we have regulated everything in their lives as is done by wise parents who desire to train children in the cause of duty and submission. For the peoples of the world in regard to the secrets of our polity are ever through the ages only children under age, precisely as are also their governments.

21. As you see, I found our despotism on right and duty: the right to compel the execution of duty is the direct obligation of a government which is a father for its subjects. It has the right of the strong that it may use it for the benefit of directing humanity towards that order which is defined by nature, namely, submission. Everything in the world is in a state of submission, if not to man, then to circumstances or its own inner character, in all cases, to what is stronger. And so shall we be this something stronger for the sake of good.

22. We are obliged without hesitation to sacrifice individuals, who commit a breach of established order, for in the exemplary punishment of evil lies a great educational problem.

23. When the King of Israel sets upon his sacred head the crown offered him by Europe he will become patriarch of the world. The indispensable victims offered by him in consequence of their suitability will never reach the number of victims offered in the course of centuries by the mania of magnificence the emulation between the GOY governments.

24. Our King will be in constant communion with the peoples, making to them from the tribune speeches which fame will in that same hour distribute over all the world.

PROTOCOL No. 16

1. In order to effect the destruction of all collective forces except ours we shall emasculate the first stage of collectivism - the UNIVERSITIES, by re-educating them in a new direction. THEIR OFFICIALS AND PROFESSORS WILL BE PREPARED FOR THEIR BUSINESS BY DETAILED SECRET PROGRAMS OF ACTION FROM WHICH THEY WILL NOT WITH IMMUNITY DIVERGE, NOT BY ONE IOTA. THEY WILL BE APPOINTED WITH ESPECIAL PRECAUTION, AND WILL BE SO PLACED AS TO BE WHOLLY DEPENDENT UPON THE GOVERNMENT.

2. We shall exclude from the course of instruction State Law as also all that concerns the political question. These subjects will be taught to a few dozen of persons chosen for their pre-eminent capacities from among the number of the initiated. THE UNIVERSITIES MUST NO LONGER SEND OUT FROM THEIR HALLS MILK SOPS CONCOCTING PLANS FOR A CONSTITUTION, LIKE A COMEDY OR A TRAGEDY, BUSYING THEMSELVES WITH QUESTIONS OF POLICY IN WHICH EVEN THEIR OWN FATHERS NEVER HAD ANY POWER OF THOUGHT.

3. The ill-guided acquaintance of a large number of persons with questions of polity creates utopian dreamers and bad subjects, as you can see for yourselves from the example of the universal education in this direction of the GOYIM. We must introduce into their education all those principles which have so brilliantly broken up their order. But when we are in power we shall remove every kind of disturbing subject from the course of education and shall make out of the youth obedient children of authority, loving him who rules as the support and hope of peace and quiet.

WE SHALL CHANGE HISTORY

4. Classicism as also any form of study of ancient history, in which there are more bad than good examples, we shall replace with the study of the program of the future. We shall erase from the memory of men all facts of previous centuries which are undesirable to us, and leave only those which depict all the errors of the government of the GOYIM. The study of practical life, of the

obligations of order, of the relations of people one to another, of avoiding bad and selfish examples, which spread the infection of evil, and similar questions of an educative nature, will stand in the forefront of the teaching program, which will be drawn up on a separate plan for each calling or state of life, in no wise generalizing the teaching. This treatment of the question has special importance.

5. Each state of life must be trained within strict limits corresponding to its destination and work in life. The OCCASIONAL GENIUS HAS ALWAYS MANAGED AND ALWAYS WILL MANAGE TO SLIP THROUGH INTO OTHER STATES OF LIFE, BUT IT IS THE MOST PERFECT FOLLY FOR THE SAKE OF THIS RARE OCCASIONAL GENIUS TO LET THROUGH INTO RANKS FOREIGN TO THEM THE UNTALENTED WHO THUS ROB OF THEIR PLACES THOSE WHO BELONG TO THOSE RANKS BY BIRTH OR EMPLOYMENT. YOU KNOW YOURSELVES IN WHAT ALL THIS HAS ENDED FOR THE "GOYIM" WHO ALLOWED THIS CRYING ABSURDITY.

6. In order that he who rules may be seated firmly in the hearts and minds of his subjects it is necessary for the time of his activity to instruct the whole nation in the schools and on the market places about this meaning and his acts and all his beneficent initiatives.

7. We shall abolish every kind of freedom of instruction. Learners of all ages have the right to assemble together with their parents in the educational establishments as it were in a club: during these assemblies, on holidays, teachers will read what will pass as free lectures on questions of human relations, of the laws of examples, of the philosophy of new theories not yet declared to the world. These theories will be raised by us to the stage of a dogma of faith as a traditional stage towards our faith. On the completion of this exposition of our program of action in the present and the future I will read you the principles of these theories.

8. In a word, knowing by the experience of many centuries that people live and are guided by ideas, that these ideas are imbided by people only by the aid of education provided with equal success for all ages of growth, but of course by varying methods, we shall swallow up and confiscate to our own use the last scintilla of independence of thought, which we have for long past been directing towards subjects and ideas useful for us. The system of bridling thought is already at work in the so-called system of teaching by OBJECT LESSONS, the purpose of which is to turn the GOYIM into unthinking submissive brutes waiting for things to be presented before their eyes in order

to form an idea of them .... In France, one of our best agents, Bourgeois, has already made public a new program of teaching by object lessons.

PROTOCOL No. 17

1. The practice of advocacy produces men cold, cruel, persistent, unprincipled, who in all cases take up an impersonal, purely legal standpoint. They have the inveterate habit to refer everything to its value for the defense and not to the public welfare of its results. They do not usually decline to undertake any defense whatever, they strive for an acquittal at all costs, caviling over every petty crux of jurisprudence and thereby they demoralize justice. For this reason we shall set this profession into narrow frames which will keep it inside this sphere of executive public service. Advocates, equally with judges, will be deprived of the right of communication with litigants; they will receive business only from the court and will study it by notes of report and documents, defending their clients after they have been interrogated in court on facts that have appeared. They will receive an honorarium without regard to the quality of the defense. This will render them mere reporters on law-business in the interests of justice and as counterpoise to the proctor who will be the reporter in the interests of prosecution; this will shorten business before the courts. In this way will be established a practice of honest unprejudiced defense conducted not from personal interest but by conviction. This will also, by the way, remove the present practice of corrupt bargain between advocation to agree only to let that side win which pays most .....

WE SHALL DESTROY THE CLERGY

2. WE HAVE LONG PAST TAKEN CARE TO DISCREDIT THE PRIESTHOOD OF THE *"GOYIM,"* and thereby to ruin their mission on earth which in these days might still be a great hindrance to us. Day by day its influence on the peoples of the world is falling lower. FREEDOM OF CONSCIENCE HAS BEEN DECLARED EVERYWHERE, SO THAT NOW ONLY YEARS DIVIDE US FROM THE MOMENT OF THE COMPLETE WRECKING OF THAT CHRISTIAN RELIGION: as to other religions we shall have still less difficulty in dealing with them, but it would be premature to speak of this now. We shall set clericalism and clericals into such narrow frames as to make their influence move in retrogressive proportion to its former progress.

3. When the time comes finally to destroy the papal court the finger of an invisible hand will point the nations towards this court. When, however, the nations fling themselves upon it, we shall come forward in the guise of its defenders as if to save excessive bloodshed. By this diversion we shall penetrate

to its very bowels and be sure we shall never come out again until we have gnawed through the entire strength of this place.

4. THE KING OF THE JEWS WILL BE THE REAL POPE OF THE UNIVERSE, THE PATRIARCH OF THE INTERNATIONAL CHURCH

5. But, IN THE MEANTIME, while we are re-educating youth in new traditional religions and afterwards in ours, WE SHALL NOT OVERTLY LAY A FINGER ON EXISTING CHURCHES, BUT WE SHALL FIGHT AGAINST THEM BY CRITICISM CALCULATED TO PRODUCE SCHISM . . .

6. In general, then, our contemporary press will continue to CONVICT State affairs, religions, incapacities of the GOYIM, always using the most unprincipled expressions in order by every means to lower their prestige in the manner which can only be practiced by the genius of our gifted tribe . . . *(Calling the Jim Jones massacre in Guyana a mass suicide, not a C.I.A./MK-ULTRA/U.S. Government massacre? Denying the massacre of the Branch Dravidian sect at Waco, Texas, was a needless and deliberate massacre by the B.A.T.F./F.B.I/C.I.A/U.S. Government).*

7. Our kingdom will be an apologia of the divinity Vishnu, in whom is found its personification - in our hundred hands will be, one in each, the springs of the machinery of social life. We shall see everything without the aid of official police which, in that scope of its rights which we elaborated for the use of the GOYIM, hinders governments from seeing. In our programs ONE-THIRD OF OUR SUBJECTS WILL KEEP THE REST UNDER OBSERVATION from a sense of duty, on the principle of volunteer service to the State. It will then be no disgrace to be a spy and informer, but a merit: unfounded denunciations, however, will be cruelly punished that there may be no development of abuses of this right.

8. Our agents will be taken from the higher as well as the lower ranks of society, from among the administrative class who spend their time in amusements, editors, printers and publishers, booksellers, clerks, and salesmen, workmen, coachmen, lackeys, et cetera. This body, having no rights and not being empowered to take any action on their own account, and consequently a police without any power, will only witness and report: verification of their reports and arrests will depend upon a responsible group of controllers of police affairs, while the actual act of arrest will be performed by the gendarmerie and the municipal police. Any person not denouncing anything

seen or heard concerning questions of polity will also be charged with and made responsible for concealment, if it be proved that he is guilty of this crime.

9. JUST AS NOWADAYS OUR BRETHREN, ARE OBLIGED AT THEIR OWN RISK TO DENOUNCE TO THE KAHAL APOSTATES OF THEIR OWN FAMILY or members who have been noticed doing anything in opposition to the KAHAL, SO IN OUR KINGDOM OVER ALL THE WORLD IT WILL BE OBLIGATORY FOR ALL OUR SUBJECTS TO OBSERVE THE DUTY OF SERVICE TO THE STATE IN THIS DIRECTION.

10. Such an organization will extirpate abuses of authority, of force, of bribery, everything in fact which we by our counsels, by our theories of the superhuman rights of man, have introduced into the customs of the GOYIM .... But how else were we to procure that increase of causes predisposing to disorders in the midst of their administration? .... Among the number of those methods one of the most important is - agents for the restoration of order, so placed as to have the opportunity in their disintegrating activity of developing and displaying their evil inclinations - obstinate self-conceit, irresponsible exercise of authority, and, first and foremost, venality. *(Janet Reno? B.A.T.F.? C.I.A.?)*

PROTOCOL No. 18

1. When it becomes necessary for us to strengthen the strict measures of secret defense (the most fatal poison for the prestige of authority) we shall arrange a simulation of disorders or some manifestation of discontents finding expression through the co-operation of good speakers. Round these speakers will assemble all who are sympathetic to his utterances. This will give us the pretext for domiciliary prerequisitions and surveillance on the part of our servants from among the number of the GOYIM police ... *(Australia's One Nation Party? A.D.L./B'nai B'rith activities against the peace?)*

2. As the majority of conspirators act out of love for the game, for the sake of talking, so, until they commit some overt act we shall not lay a finger on them but only introduce into their midst observation elements .... It must be remembered that the prestige of authority is lessened if it frequently discovers conspiracies against itself: this implies a presumption of consciousness of weakness, or, what is still worse, of injustice. You are aware that we have broken the prestige of the GOY kings by frequent attempts upon their lives through our agents, blind sheep of our flock, who are easily moved by a few liberal phrases to crimes provided only they be painted in political colors. WE HAVE COMPELLED THE RULERS TO ACKNOWLEDGE THEIR WEAKNESS IN ADVERTISING OVERT MEASURES OF SECRET

DEFENSE AND THEREBY WE SHALL BRING THE PROMISE OF AUTHORITY TO DESTRUCTION.

3. Our ruler will be secretly protected only by the most insignificant guard, because we shall not admit so much as a thought that there could exist against him any sedition with which he is not strong enough to contend and is compelled to hide from it.

4. If we should admit this thought, as the GOYIM have done and are doing, we should IPSO FACTO be signing a death sentence, if not for our ruler, at any rate for his dynasty, at no distant date.

GOVERNMENT BY FEAR

5. According to strictly enforced outward appearances our ruler will employ his power only for the advantage of the nation and in no wise for his own or dynastic profits. Therefore, with the observance of this decorum, his authority will be respected and guarded by the subjects themselves, it will receive an apotheosis in the admission that with it is bound up the well-being of every citizen of the State, for upon it will depend all order in the common life of the pack ....

6. OVERT DEFENSE OF THE KIND ARGUES WEAKNESS IN THE ORGANIZATION OF HIS STRENGTH.

7. Our ruler will always be among the people and be surrounded by a mob of apparently curious men and women, who will occupy the front ranks about him, to all appearance by chance, and will restrain the ranks of the rest out of respect as it will appear for good order. This will sow an example of restraint also in others. If a petitioner appears among the people trying to hand a petition and forcing his way through the ranks, the first ranks must receive the petition and before the eyes of the petitioner pass it to the ruler, so that all may know that what is handed in reaches its destination, that consequently, there exists a control of the ruler himself. The aureole of power requires for his existence that the people may be able to say: *"If the king knew of this,"* or: *"the king will hear it."*

8. WITH THE ESTABLISHMENT OF OFFICIAL DEFENSE, THE MYSTICAL PRESTIGE OF AUTHORITY DISAPPEARS: given a certain audacity, and everyone counts himself master of it, the sedition-monger is conscious of his strength, and when occasion serves watches for the moment to make an attempt upon authority .... For the GOYIM we have been preaching

something else, but by that very fact we are enabled to see what measures of overt defense have brought them to ....

9. CRIMINALS WITH US WILL BE ARRESTED AT THE FIRST, more or less, well-grounded SUSPICION: it cannot be allowed that out of fear of a possible mistake an opportunity should be given of escape to persons suspected of a political lapse of crime, for in these matters we shall be literally merciless. If it is still possible, by stretching a point, to admit a reconsideration of the motive causes in simple crimes, there is no possibility of excuse for persons occupying themselves with questions in which nobody except the government can understand anything .... And it is not all governments that understand true policy.

PROTOCOL No. 19

1. If we do not permit any independent dabbling in the political we shall on the other hand encourage every kind of report or petition with proposals for the government to examine into all kinds of projects for the amelioration of the condition of the people; this will reveal to us the defects or else the fantasies of our subjects, to which we shall respond either by accomplishing them or by a wise rebuttment to prove the shortsightedness of one who judges wrongly.

2. Sedition-mongering is nothing more than the yapping of a lap-dog at an elephant. For a government well organized, not from the police but from the public point of view, the lap-dog yaps at the elephant in entire unconsciousness of its strength and importance. It needs no more than to take a good example to show the relative importance of both and the lap-dogs will cease to yap and will wag their tails the moment they set eyes on an elephant.

3. In order to destroy the prestige of heroism for political crime we shall send it for trial in the category of thieving, murder, and every kind of abominable and filthy crime. Public opinion will then confuse in its conception this category of crime with the disgrace attaching to every other and will brand it with the same contempt.

4. We have done our best, and I hope we have succeeded to obtain that the GOYIM should not arrive at this means of contending with sedition. It was for this reason that through the Press and in speeches, indirectly - in cleverly compiled school-books on history, we have advertised the martyrdom alleged to have been accredited by sedition-mongers for the idea of the commonweal.

This advertisement has increased the contingent of liberals and has brought thousands of GOYIM into the ranks of our livestock cattle.

PROTOCOL No. 20

1. To-day we shall touch upon the financial program, which I put off to the end of my report as being the most difficult, the crowning and the decisive point of our plans. Before entering upon it I will remind you that I have already spoken before by way of a hint when I said that the sum total of our actions is settled by the question of figures.

2. When we come into our kingdom our autocratic government will avoid, from a principle of self-preservation, sensibly burdening the masses of the people with taxes, remembering that it plays the part of father and protector. But as State organization cost dear it is necessary nevertheless to obtain the funds required for it. It will, therefore, elaborate with particular precaution the question of equilibrium in this matter.

3. Our rule, in which the king will enjoy the legal fiction that everything in his State belongs to him *(which may easily be translated into fact)*, will be enabled to resort to the lawful confiscation of all sums of every kind for the regulation of their circulation in the State. From this follows that taxation will best be covered by a progressive tax on property. In this manner the dues will be paid without straitening or ruining anybody in the form of a percentage of the amount of property. The rich must be aware that it is their duty to place a part of their superfluities at the disposal of the State since the State guarantees them security of possession of the rest of their property and the right of honest gains, I say honest, for the control over property will do away with robbery on a legal basis.

4. This social reform must come from above, for the time is ripe for it - it is indispensable as a pledge of peace.

WE SHALL DESTROY CAPITAL

5. The tax upon the poor man is a seed of revolution and works to the detriment of the State which in hunting after the trifling is missing the big. Quite apart from this, a tax on capitalists diminishes the growth of wealth in private hands in which we have in these days concentrated it as a counterpoise to the government strength of the GOYIM - their State finances.

6. A tax increasing in a percentage ratio to capital will give much larger revenue than the present individual or property tax, which is useful to us now for the sole reason that it excites trouble and discontent among the GOYIM. *(Now we know the purpose of the 16th Amendment!!)*

7. The force upon which our king will rest consists in the equilibrium and the guarantee of peace, for the sake of which things it is indispensable that the capitalists should yield up a portion of their incomes for the sake of the secure working of the machinery of the State. State needs must be paid by those who will not feel the burden and have enough to take from.

8. Such a measure will destroy the hatred of the poor man for the rich, in whom he will see a necessary financial support for the State, will see in him the organizer of peace and well-being since he will see that it is the rich man who is paying the necessary means to attain these things.

9. In order that payers of the educated classes should not too much distress themselves over the new payments they will have full accounts given them of the destination of those payments, with the exception of such sums as will be appropriated for the needs of the throne and the administrative institutions.

10. He who reigns will not have any properties of his own once all in the State represented his patrimony, or else the one would be in contradiction to the other; the fact of holding private means would destroy the right of property in the common possessions of all.

11. Relatives of him who reigns, his heirs excepted, who will be maintained by the resources of the State, must enter the ranks of servants of the State or must work to obtain the right to property; the privilege of royal blood must not serve for the spoiling of the treasury.

12. Purchase, receipt of money or inheritance will be subject to the payment of a stamp progressive tax. Any transfer of property, whether money or other, without evidence of payment of this tax which will be strictly registered by names, will render the former holder liable to pay interest on the tax from the moment of transfer of these sums up to the discovery of his evasion of declaration of the transfer. Transfer documents must be presented weekly at the local treasury office with notifications of the name, surname and permanent place of residence of the former and the new holder of the property. This transfer with register of names must begin from a definite sum which exceeds the ordinary expenses of buying and selling necessaries, and these will be subject to payment only by a stamp impost of a definite percentage of the unit.

13. Just strike an estimate of how many times such taxes as these will cover the revenue of the GOYIM States.

WE CAUSE DEPRESSIONS

14. The State exchequer will have to maintain a definite complement of reserve sums, and all that is collected above that complement must be returned into circulation. On these sums will be organized public works. The initiative in works of this kind, proceeding from State sources, will bind the working class firmly to the interests of the State and to those who reign. From these same sums also a part will be set aside as rewards of inventiveness and productiveness.

15. On no account should so much as a single unit above the definite and freely estimated sums be retained in the State Treasuries, for money exists to be circulated and any kind of stagnation of money acts ruinously on the running of the State machinery, for which it is the lubricant; a stagnation of the lubricant may stop the regular working of the mechanism.

16. The substitution of interest-bearing paper for a part of the token of exchange has produced exactly this stagnation. The consequences of this circumstance are already sufficiently noticeable.

17. A court of account will also be instituted by us, and in it the ruler will find at any moment a full accounting for State income and expenditure, with the exception of the current monthly account, not yet made up, and that of the preceding month, which will not yet have been delivered.

18. The one and only person who will have no interest in robbing the State is its owner, the ruler. This is why his personal control will remove the possibility of leakages or extravagances.

19. The representative function of the ruler at receptions for the sake of etiquette, which absorbs so much invaluable time, will be abolished in order that the ruler may have time for control and consideration. His power will not then be split up into fractional parts among time-serving favorites who surround the throne for its pomp and splendor, and are interested only in their own and not in the common interests of the State.

20. Economic crises have been produced by us for the GOYIM by no other means than the withdrawal of money from circulation. Huge capitals have stagnated, withdrawing money from States, which were constantly obliged to

apply to those same stagnant capitals for loans. These loans burdened the finances of the State with the payment of interest and made them the bond slaves of these capitals .... The concentration of industry in the hands of capitalists out of the hands of small masters has drained away all the juices of the peoples and with them also the States .... *(Now we know the purpose of the Federal Reserve Bank Corporation!!)*

21. The present issue of money in general does not correspond with the requirements per head, and cannot therefore satisfy all the needs of the workers. The issue of money ought to correspond with the growth of population and thereby children also must absolutely be reckoned as consumers of currency from the day of their birth. The revision of issue is a material question for the whole world.

22. YOU ARE AWARE THAT THE GOLD STANDARD HAS BEEN THE RUIN OF THE STATES WHICH ADOPTED IT, FOR IT HAS NOT BEEN ABLE TO SATISFY THE DEMANDS FOR MONEY, THE MORE SO THAT WE HAVE REMOVED GOLD FROM CIRCULATION AS FAR AS POSSIBLE.

GENTILE STATES BANKRUPT

23. With us the standard that must be introduced is the cost of working-man power, whether it be reckoned in paper or in wood. We shall make the issue of money in accordance with the normal requirements of each subject, adding to the quantity with every birth and subtracting with every death.

24. The accounts will be managed by each department *(the French administrative division)*, each circle.

25. In order that there may be no delays in the paying out of money for State needs the sums and terms of such payments will be fixed by decree of the ruler; this will do away with the protection by a ministry of one institution to the detriment of others.

26. The budgets of income and expenditure will be carried out side by side that they may not be obscured by distance one to another.

27. The reforms projected by us in the financial institutions and principles of the GOYIM will be clothed by us in such forms as will alarm nobody. We shall point out the necessity of reforms in consequence of the disorderly darkness into which the GOYIM by their irregularities have plunged the

finances. The first irregularity, as we shall point out, consists in their beginning with drawing up a single budget which year after year grows owing to the following cause: this budget is dragged out to half the year, then they demand a budget to put things right, and this they expend in three months, after which they ask for a supplementary budget, and all this ends with a liquidation budget. But, as the budget of the following year is drawn up in accordance with the sum of the total addition, the annual departure from the normal reaches as much as 50 per cent in a year, and so the annual budget is trebled in ten years. Thanks to such methods, allowed by the carelessness of the GOY States, their treasuries are empty. The period of loans supervenes, and that has swallowed up remainders and brought all the GOY States to bankruptcy. (The United States was declared *"bankrupt"* at the Geneva Convention of 1929! [see 31 USC 5112, 5118, and 5119).

28. You understand perfectly that economic arrangements of this kind, which have been suggested to the GOYIM by us, cannot be carried on by us.

29. Every kind of loan proves infirmity in the State and a want of understanding of the rights of the State. Loans hang like a sword of Damocles over the heads of rulers, who, instead of taking from their subjects by a temporary tax, come begging with outstretched palm to our bankers. Foreign loans are leeches which there is no possibility of removing from the body of the State until they fall off of themselves or the State flings them off. But the GOY States do not tear them off; they go on in persisting in putting more on to themselves so that they must inevitably perish, drained by voluntary blood-letting.

TYRANNY OF USURY

30. What also indeed is, in substance, a loan, especially a foreign loan? A loan is - an issue of government bills of exchange containing a percentage obligation commensurate to the sum of the loan capital. If the loan bears a charge of 5 per cent, then in twenty years the State vainly pays away in interest a sum equal to the loan borrowed, in forty years it is paying a double sum, in sixty - treble, and all the while the debt remains an unpaid debt.

31. From this calculation it is obvious that with any form of taxation per head the State is baling out the last coppers of the poor taxpayers in order to settle accounts with wealthy foreigners, from whom it has borrowed money instead of collecting these coppers for its own needs without the additional interest.

32. So long as loans were internal the GOYIM only shuffled their money from the pockets of the poor to those of the rich, but when we bought up the necessary persons in order to transfer loans into the external sphere, *(Woodrow Wilson and F.D. Roosevelt)* all the wealth of States flowed into our cash-boxes and all the GOYIM began to pay us the tribute of subjects.

33. If the superficiality of GOY kings on their thrones in regard to State affairs and the venality of ministers or the want of understanding of financial matters on the part of other ruling persons have made their countries debtors to our treasuries to amounts quite impossible to pay it has not been accomplished without, on our part, heavy expenditure of trouble and money.

34. Stagnation of money will not be allowed by us and therefore there will be no State interest-bearing paper, except a one per-cent series, so that there will be no payment of interest to leeches that suck all the strength out of the State. The right to issue interest-bearing paper will be given exclusively to industrial companies who find no difficulty in paying interest out of profits, whereas the State does not make interest on borrowed money like these companies, for the State borrows to spend and not to use in operations. *(Now we know why President Kennedy was assassinated in 1963 when he refused to borrow any more of the "Bank Notes" from the bankers of the Federal Reserve Bank and began circulating non-interest bearing "Notes" of the "United States of America"!!!).*

35. Industrial papers will be bought also by the government which from being as now a paper of tribute by loan operations will be transformed into a lender of money at a profit. This measure will stop the stagnation of money, parasitic profits and idleness, all of which were useful for us among the GOYIM so long as they were independent but are not desirable under our rule.

36. How clear is the undeveloped power of thought of the purely brute brains of the GOYIM, as expressed in the fact that they have been borrowing from us with payment of interest without ever thinking that all the same these very moneys plus an addition for payment of interest must be got by them from their own State pockets in order to settle up with us. What could have been simpler than to take the money they wanted from their own people?

37. But it is a proof of the genius of our chosen mind that we have contrived to present the matter of loans to them in such a light that they have even seen in them an advantage for themselves.

38. Our accounts, which we shall present when the time comes, in the light of centuries of experience gained by experiments made by us on the GOY States, will be distinguished by clearness and definiteness and will show at a glance to all men the advantage of our innovations. They will put an end to those abuses to which we owe our mastery over the GOYIM, but which cannot be allowed in our kingdom.

39. We shall so hedge about our system of accounting that neither the ruler nor the most insignificant public servant will be in a position to divert even the smallest sum from its destination without detection or to direct it in another direction except that which will be once fixed in a definite plan of action. *(Is this why a "private corporation," known as the "Internal Revenue Service," is in charge of collecting the "payments" of the "Income Taxes" and the IRS always deposits those "payments" to the Federal Reserve bank and never to the Treasury of the United States??)*

40. And without a definite plan it is impossible to rule. Marching along an undetermined road and with undetermined resources brings to ruin by the way heroes and demi-gods.

41. The GOY rulers, whom we once upon a time advised should be distracted from State occupations by representative receptions, observances of etiquette, entertainments, were only screens for our rule. *(Like the House of Windsor (Guelph) and the rest of the "Black Nobility"?)* The accounts of favorite courtiers who replaced them in the sphere of affairs were drawn up for them by our agents, and every time gave satisfaction to short-sighted minds by promises that in the future economies and improvements were foreseen .... Economies from what? From new taxes? - were questions that might have been but were not asked by those who read our accounts and projects.

42. You know to what they have been brought by this carelessness, to what pitch of financial disorder they have arrived, notwithstanding the astonishing industry of their peoples ....

PROTOCOL No. 21

1. To what I reported to you at the last meeting I shall now add a detailed explanation of internal loans. Of foreign loans I shall say nothing more, because they have fed us with the national moneys of the GOYIM, but for our State there will be no foreigners, that is, nothing external.

2. We have taken advantage of the venality of administrators and slackness of rulers to get our moneys twice, thrice and more times over, by lending to the GOY governments moneys which were not at all needed by the States. Could anyone do the like in regard to us? .... Therefore, I shall only deal with the details of internal loans.

3. States announce that such a loan is to be concluded and open subscriptions for their own bills of exchange, that is, for their interest-bearing paper. That they may be within the reach of all the price is determined at from a hundred to a thousand; and a discount is made for the earliest subscribers. Next day by artificial means the price of them goes up, the alleged reason being that everyone is rushing to buy them. In a few days the treasury safes are, as they say, overflowing and there's more money than they can do with *(why then take it?)* The subscription, it is alleged, covers many times over the issue total of the loan; in this lies the whole stage effect - look you, they say, what confidence is shown in the government's bills of exchange.

4. But when the comedy is played out there emerges the fact that a debit and an exceedingly burdensome debit has been created. For the payment of interest it becomes necessary to have recourse to new loans, which do not swallow up but only add to the capital debt. And when this credit is exhausted it becomes necessary by new taxes to cover, not the loan, BUT ONLY THE INTEREST ON IT. These taxes are a debit employed to cover a debit .... *(Hence THE CRY TO BALANCE THE BUDGET!)*

5. Later comes the time for conversions, but they diminish the payment of interest without covering the debt, and besides they cannot be made without the consent of the lenders; on announcing a conversion a proposal is made to return the money to those who are not willing to convert their paper. If everybody expressed his unwillingness and demanded his money back, the government would be hoist on their own petard and would be found insolvent and unable to pay the proposed sums. By good luck the subjects of the GOY governments, knowing nothing about financial affairs, have always preferred losses on exchange and diminution of interest to the risk of new investments of their moneys, and have thereby many a time enabled these governments to throw off their shoulders a debit of several millions.

6. Nowadays, with external loans, these tricks cannot be played by the GOYIM for they know that we shall demand all our moneys back.

7. In this way in acknowledged bankruptcy will best prove to the various countries the absence of any means between the interests of the peoples and of those who rule them.

8. I beg you to concentrate your particular attention upon this point and upon the following: nowadays all internal loans are consolidated by so-called flying loans, that is, such as have terms of payment more or less near. These debts consist of moneys paid into the savings banks and reserve funds. If left for long at the disposition of a government these funds evaporate in the payment of interest on foreign loans, and are placed by the deposit of equivalent amount of RENTS.

9. And these last it is which patch up all the leaks in the State treasuries of the GOYIM.

10. When we ascend the throne of the world all these financial and similar shifts, as being not in accord with our interests, will be swept away so as not to leave a trace, as also will be destroyed all money markets, since we shall not allow the prestige of our power to be shaken by fluctuations of prices set upon our values, which we shall announce by law at the price which represents their full worth without any possibility of lowering or raising. *(Raising gives the pretext for lowering, which indeed was where we made a beginning in relation to the values of the GOYIM).*

11. We shall replace the money markets by grandiose government credit institutions, the object of which will be to fix the price of industrial values in accordance with government views. These institutions will be in a position to fling upon the market five hundred millions of industrial paper in one day, or to buy up for the same amount. In this way all industrial undertakings will come into dependence upon us. You may imagine for yourselves what immense power we shall thereby secure for ourselves ....

PROTOCOL No. 22

1 In all that has so far been reported by me to you, I have endeavored to depict with care the secret of what is coming, of what is past, and of what is going on now, rushing into the flood of the great events coming already in the near future, the secret of our relations to the GOYIM and of financial operations. On this subject there remains still a little for me to add.

2. IN OUR HANDS IS THE GREATEST POWER OF OUR DAY - GOLD: IN TWO DAYS WE CAN PROCURE FROM OUR STOREHOUSES ANY QUANTITY WE MAY PLEASE.

3. Surely there is no need to seek further proof that our rule is predestined by God? Surely we shall not fail with such wealth to prove that all that evil which

for so many centuries we have had to commit has served at the end of ends the cause of true well-being - the bringing of everything into order? Though it be even by the exercise of some violence, yet all the same it will be established. *(The motto of the Freemasons - "Out of Chaos, Order").* We shall contrive to prove that we are benefactors who have restored to the rent and mangled earth the true good and also freedom of the person, and therewith we shall enable it to be enjoyed in peace and quiet, with proper dignity of relations, on the condition, of course, of strict observance of the laws established by us. We shall make plain therewith that freedom does not consist in dissipation and in the right of unbridled license any more than the dignity and force of a man do not consist in the right of everyone to promulgate destructive principles in the nature of freedom of conscience, equality and the like, that freedom of the person in no wise consists in the right to agitate oneself and others by abominable speeches before disorderly mobs, and that true freedom consists in the inviolability of the person who honorably and strictly observes all the laws of life in common, that human dignity is wrapped up in consciousness of the rights and also of the absence of rights of each, and not wholly and solely in fantastic imaginings about the subject of one's EGO.

4. One authority will be glorious because it will be all-powerful, will rule and guide, and not muddle along after leaders and orators shrieking themselves hoarse with senseless words which they call great principles and which are nothing else, to speak honestly, but utopian .... Our authority will be the crown of order, and in that is included the whole happiness of man. The aureole of this authority will inspire a mystical bowing of the knee before it and a reverent fear before it of all the peoples. True force makes no terms with any right, not even with that of God: none dare come near to it so as to take so much as a span from it away.

PROTOCOL No. 23

I. That the peoples may become accustomed to obedience it is necessary to inculcate lessons of humility and therefore to reduce the production of articles of luxury. By this we shall improve morals which have been debased by emulation in the sphere of luxury. We shall re-establish small master production which will mean laying a mine under the private capital of manufactures. This is indispensable also for the reason that manufacturers on the grand scale often move, though not always consciously, the thoughts of the masses in directions against the government. A people of small masters knows nothing of unemployment and this binds him closely with existing order, and consequently with the firmness of authority. For us its part will have been played out the moment authority is transferred into our hands. Drunkenness

138

also will be prohibited by law and punishable as a crime against the humanness of man who is turned into a brute under the influence of alcohol.

2. Subjects, I repeat once more, give blind obedience only to the strong hand which is absolutely independent of them, for in it they feel the sword of defense and support against social scourges .... What do they want with an angelic spirit in a king? What they have to see in him is the personification of force and power.

3. The supreme lord who will replace all now existing rulers, dragging in their existence among societies demoralized by us, societies that have denied even the authority of God, from whose midst breeds out on all sides the fire of anarchy, must first of all proceed to quench this all-devouring flame. Therefore he will be obliged to kill off those existing societies, though he should drench them with his own blood, that he may resurrect them again in the form of regularly organized troops fighting consciously with every kind of infection that may cover the body of the State with sores.

4. This Chosen One of God is chosen from above to demolish the senseless forces moved by instinct and not reason, by brutishness and not humanness. These forces now triumph in manifestations of robbery and every kind of violence under the mask of principles of freedom and rights. They have overthrown all forms of social order to erect on the ruins the throne of the King of the Jews; but their part will be played out the moment he enters into his kingdom. Then it will be necessary to sweep them away from his path, on which must be left no knot, no splinter.

5. Then will it be possible for us to say to the peoples of the world: "Give thanks to God and bow the knee before him who bears on his front the seal of the predestination of man, to which God himself has led his star that none other but Him might free us from all the before-mentioned forces and evils".

PROTOCOL No. 24

1. I pass now to the method of confirming the dynastic roots of King David to the last strata of the earth.

2. This confirmation will first and foremost be included in that which to this day has rested the force of conservatism by our learned elders of the conduct of the affairs of the world, in the directing of the education of thought of all humanity.

3. Certain members of the seed of David will prepare the kings and their heirs, selecting not by right of heritage but by eminent capacities, inducting them into the most secret mysteries of the political, into schemes of government, but providing always that none may come to knowledge of the secrets. The object of this mode of action is that all may know that government cannot be entrusted to those who have not been inducted into the secret places of its art ....

4. To these persons only will be taught the practical application of the aforenamed plans by comparison of the experiences of many centuries, all the observations on the politico-economic moves and social sciences - in a word, all the spirit of laws which have been unshakably established by nature herself for the regulation of the relations of humanity.

5. Direct heirs will often be set aside from ascending the throne if in their time of training they exhibit frivolity, softness and other qualities that are the ruin of authority, which render them incapable of governing and in themselves dangerous for kingly office.

6. Only those who are unconditionally capable for firm, even if it be to cruelty, direct rule will receive the reins of rule from our learned elders.

7. In case of falling sick with weakness of will or other form of incapacity. kings must by law hand over the reins of rule to new and capable hands.

8. The king's plan of action for the current moment, and all the more so for the future, will be unknown, even to those who are called his closest counselors.

KING OF THE JEWS

9. Only the king and the three who stood sponsor for him will know what is coming.

10. In the person of the king who with unbending will is master of himself and of humanity all will discern as it were fate with its mysterious ways. None will know what the king wishes to attain by his dispositions, and therefore none will dare to stand across an unknown path.

11. It is understood that the brain reservoir of the king must correspond in capacity to the plan of government it has to contain. It is for this reason that

he will ascend the throne not otherwise than after examination of his mind by the aforesaid learned elders.

12. That the people may know and love their king, it is indispensable for him to converse in the market-places with his people. This ensures the necessary clinching of the two forces which are now divided one from another by us by the terror.

13. This terror was indispensable for us till the time comes for both these forces separately to fall under our influence.

14. The king of the Jews must not be at the mercy of his passions, and especially of sensuality: on no side of his character must he give brute instincts power over his mind. Sensuality worse than all else disorganizes the capacities of the mind and clearness of views, distracting the thoughts to the worst and most brutal side of human activity.

15. The prop of humanity in the person of the supreme lord of all the world of the holy seed of David must sacrifice to his people all personal inclinations.

16. Our supreme lord must be of an exemplary irreproachability.

Signed by the representative of
Zion, of the 33rd Degree